GRAHAM LANCASTER

# THE 20% FACTOR

## The key to personal and corporate success

A GRAHAM TARRANT BOOK

**DAVID & CHARLES**

Newton Abbot    London    North Pomfret (Vt)

For Terry Lambert

The author and publishers gratefully acknowledge permission to
quote from the following works in copyright: *Human Engineering*
by Lord Robens, published by Jonathan Cape Ltd (by kind
permission of St Paul's Bibliographies); *Communicating in Organizations* by Gerald M. Phillips, reprinted with permission of
Macmillan Publishing Company, New York, copyright © 1982;
'Letters from a keen young marketing man', by permission of
*Campaign* magazine.

**British Library Cataloguing in Publication Data**

Lancaster, Graham
  The 20% factor: the key to personal
  and corporate success. – (A Graham
  Tarrant book).
  1. Success
  I. Title
  158'.1    BF637.S8

  ISBN 0-7153-8867-3

Typeset by Typesetters (Birmingham) Ltd,
Smethwick, West Midlands
and printed in Great Britain
by Redwood Burn Limited, Trowbridge, Wilts
for David & Charles Publishers plc
Brunel House  Newton Abbot  Devon

Published in the United States of America
by David & Charles Inc
North Pomfret  Vermont 05053  USA

# The Twenty Per Cent Factor

You can improve yourself in business and social life by twenty per cent almost overnight. Twenty per cent greater salary, sales, profits, satisfaction, prospects of promotion and security are all there for the taking.

This is The Twenty Per Cent Factor that new management brooms, consultants, trainers, psychologists and other relative outsiders go for and generally deliver as part of their magic. Rapid improvements much beyond this are subject to diminishing returns and depend on basics which need more fundamental work or which are largely outside anyone's control.

This book is not concerned with the breathless pursuit of excellence. The constant flow of 'look at me, Ma' books from tycoons and consultants can seriously damage your confidence. Aiming for management superstar status is by definition a sensible goal only for the very, very few. For you and me, the majority, to compare ourselves with them, to try and emulate them, is simply to court failure against far too ambitious a target.

Take up your twenty per cent of slack, however, really settle into your new much improved level of performance and something wonderful happens. Another twenty becomes possible, so that over a reasonable period of time that goal of excellence really does come within reach. There is another benefit. This steady ratcheting up of improvements seems acceptable and unthreatening to others, whereas the wide-eyed new convert to the idol of excellence only attracts resentment, ridicule and opposition.

There are a variety of twenty per cents to be claimed in an organisational sense. Better credit control and cash flow management; materials handling; quality control; distribution; training and so on.

*You* however are the easiest target of all – in your personal life and in terms of contribution to your organisation, be it office, factory or home. Know yourself, what you want and what others want from you, and you can package yourself, your product or organisation far more effectively.

There are strong parallels in the way we talk about people, products and organisations. We talk about an individual's personality, about brand personalities and about corporate personalities. We talk about dress sense, about product packaging, and about architecture and interior design. By using a mix of successful techniques from the social skills and from brand and corporate management, remarkable results can be achieved. We can package and market *ourselves* better, and in turn give our products and companies the kind of human characteristics which research tells us will lead to success.

This is not a traditional marketing or public relations handbook, many of which can already be found on the bookshelves. It is altogether more ambitious than that.

Instead it aims to expose and help you change damaging attitudes and images, and to help you create a far better climate in which you, your product and your organisation can prosper.

First impressions and presentation are vital and *The 20% Factor* gives the blunt, sometimes barely palatable advice you need to put your very best face forward.

# PART ONE
## Knowing Yourself

# First Impressions Last

One or two seconds. That's how long it takes for people important to you to arrive at their opinion of you as a person, or of your product or organisation.

This is not merely a first impression – although it is that as well – but their whole opinion. Anything you do or say after these first seconds may help strengthen this opinion, or begin the long and difficult job of changing it. Just to make things even more difficult, research shows how important non-rational and emotional factors are in this complex process of opinion forming – often outweighing rational assessment.

'We got off on the wrong foot.'

'Customers think our product is of poor quality/unreliable/poor value/ inferior to our competitors . . . How can we burst these myths?'

'People think our company is a sleeping giant/old-fashioned/not aggressive/not successful . . . We must change these out of date views.'

Comments like these are all too common. But why start from here? Few things are more difficult than changing someone's opinion. Deep down, I don't think you ever can completely. If you *must* start from here, this book will help. For everyone, however, there are new encounters every day with important groups and the central message is to analyse and plan. How much better to appear as good as you are from the first hello. After all, you never get a second chance to make a good first impression.

You are what you seem. You will be pigeon-holed, labelled in fairly indelible ink and filed accordingly. It is the gap between how people, products and organisations would like to be seen, and how they are seen that is at the heart of so much failure, unhappiness, poor morale and disappointment – personal, professional and corporate.

The explosive growth in the public relations industry, in TV and speech training for presidents, prime ministers and chief executives, in corporate advertising and corporate design, in customer relations training and in systematic research points to the thirst for solutions.

Knowing yourself – your unique strengths and your weaknesses – knowing what you want from given situations and knowing what others want from you, are essential ingredients for success.

'Success', getting what you want, may not necessarily equate with happiness, but conscious persistent under-achievement is certainly a prime cause of frustration, depression and that aura of failure that seems to hang over some people and some corporations.

## Know Yourself

For me the world's greatest philosopher was Socrates. Partly because he had the good sense to leave behind no written works for schoolchildren to hate to learn and so learn to hate. Let young Plato get all the blame. Mostly because he dwelled on the Delphic theme of 'know thyself', perhaps the best piece of advice ever given.

Good advice is not always welcome of course. Socrates went about unfashionably promoting virtue as well as self-awareness, and they poisoned him for it. Beware of Greeks bearing grudges. Knowing yourself is certainly the first step in the Delphic business of PR.

Definitions of PR vary. To a politician it stands for proportional representation. To an art critic, pre-Raphaelite. To *West Side Story* fans, a Puerto Rican. And to the medical profession it is a branch of medicine called per rectum . . .

PR in a business sense, public relations, is the management of communications between people, products and organisations with the various groups important to them – customers, employees, shareholders, suppliers, officialdom and all the other welcome and unwelcome people who can help or hinder the achievement of corporate objectives.

Success in most important aspects of our lives is about success with people – human relationships. Our ability to make friends, to attract the opposite sex, find a spouse, to be popular, respected, get a good job and do well . . . the achievement of all of these objectives depends heavily on our own personal PR skills. Even in spheres where inter-personal skills perhaps ought not to matter so much, where technical competence or excellence ought to be the main criteria, we all know that frequently it is not so. You may be a perfectly trained word-processor operator, racing driver or concert pianist but you probably will not get the job, the car or the tour and recording contract if competing alongside you is someone with broadly similar technical skills but greater charisma, warmth, call it what you will.

One of the constant messages deliberately repeated throughout this book will be that to succeed you have to know what others want or expect from you, and that you then need to package yourself as best you can to deliver. This almost always means a degree of submissiveness and acceptance of the need to sublimate any character traits you have which, objectively, you may feel could jeopardise your chance of success. To people who began their working lives in the 1950s or earlier this kind of thinking is unexceptionable. Conforming to social and workplace conventions was the norm. Wartime service and conscription in the fifties only served to re-enforce the point.

## Blame John Lennon

To those who left school for work or university from the early 1960s, however, the whole concept of submissiveness and character sublimation is far more jarring, alien and for many, downright unacceptable. We can thank or blame the sixties for this.

I think we are only just beginning to appreciate how significant the sixties revolution really was. Not the mini-skirts and funny memorabilia from Carnaby Street, but the psychological watershed it marked for a newly created strata in society worldwide – the youth culture.

The Beatles were the catalysts for the movement, giving youth an identity and role for the first time in modern history, making young people much more than 'teenagers', trainee adults. They gave an army of baby boom young people the right to self-expression, in appearance, dress, hair, language, music, art and opinions – especially opinions on subjects like Vietnam, sex, drugs, and the establishment.

I was twenty-one when working on a summer camp in Vermont in 1969, and remember the tears and anger of some of the young people there when they heard from home that elder brothers had been conscripted for Vietnam. It was a strange summer. News was coming in from afar about British troops going into Northern Ireland (it seemed like a joke at first); just a short flight away the hippies of the world were congregating for some rock concert or other at an unheard of place called Woodstock (I decided I wouldn't bother going – just another rock concert I thought); and one night we all sat up watching a Japanese TV set to see Neil Armstrong set foot on the moon (one of the subsequent news bulletins reported celebrations in Germany equal to those in the States, claiming it was wartime German rocket technology that got them there).

Wearing love beads and milking my northern English accent for all it was worth, I remember just how infectious the spirit of the rebellious youth movement was. American summer camps are run on quasi-military lines, getting up, eating and lights out to recorded bugle instructions, and the adult camp directors and some of the dreaded senior counsellors (mostly experienced teachers) were the butt for most of our frustrations. Recently I found in a diary a poem I wrote at the time, which captures the mood many of us had of impotent, immature anger:

*It's not the endless boredom,*
*Nor the mood of hate,*
*The feeling of rage,*
*The goad of the bait.*
*Not the bovine screams,*
*Of these children in hell.*
*Nor the 'Blood Sweat and Tears',*
*The bugle the bell.*
*But these big little men,*
*In this world for the small.*
*These big little men,*
*Who for two months walk tall.*

One of the young Americans, aged around nineteen, described to me at the time the impact the Beatles thing had had on his life and that of his peers. Before them, the American middle-class teenage boy had a crew-cut and was really seen as an apprentice adult. Sure he could play with a baseball mitt, throw basket balls in the yard and drink sodas, but in terms of dress and behaviour, in terms of manners and opinions, his cue was to emulate the values of his parents. If he did that, he was well on his way to success, to college and a career. After the Beatles the tip of the iceberg shown by the likes of James Dean in *Rebel Without a Cause*, and which had been just hinted at by some of the late 1950s white rock and rollers (especially Elvis Presley and Jerry Lee Lewis), was seen to be far more threatening than anticipated. Longer hair and non-conformist dress were the first signs, which led to family fights, which led to greater polarisation and all that has followed in its wake. Benjamin – Dustin Hoffman in the film *The Graduate* – would have taken his family friend's advice to go into 'plastics' a few years earlier, and would probably have been happier as a result.

As someone who, despite a quarter of a century's hyperbole, thinks the Beatles' work has been underrated, as someone who still blinks hard when listening to John Lennon's last album, I have to say that I think the influence of the Beatles and all the cult of the individual that followed has been on the whole disastrous. Genius has always been able to afford eccentricities – Mozart, Gauguin – which lesser genius probably could not – Bruckner, Sisley. As for you and me? We can admire the eccentricity of great or popular talent, but the real mistake from the 1960s was the belief that copying the eccentricities of those we admired was somehow acceptable.

American folk singer, Suzanne Vega, was quoted in the *London Standard* as saying: 'I suppose what annoys me the most about Madonna (the pop singer) is her lack of responsibility. All the little girls who like her and dress like her aren't going to grow up rich and famous like her, they're going to grow up to be treated like tramps.'

We have to unlearn the cult of individualism, which is still kept alive by so many middle-aged sixties people and their disciples in the still less rigid worlds of entertainment, literature, advertising, journalism, broadcasting, further education, cinema and the arts – some of the few remaining areas where cautious bohemianism is still acceptable. We have to realise that bosses want to feel safe if they put us on their corporate mantelpiece. We have to re-learn the traditions that were second nature before then. To quote H. Gordon Selfridge, the customer *is* always right, and a customer for your services by any other name is called a boss. Give them what they want. Find out what style of approach the other person wants, what style of management if it is a company they prefer, and present yourself as the solution. Highlight a demand in their minds that you can meet.

## Trained Alsatians

Knowing what your objectives are and knowing the influences upon a business (knowing yourself) comes intuitively to natural entrepreneurs. These things are always at the top of their minds. I remember I once asked the boss of a small clothing firm what he made – meaning raincoats, trousers, dressing gowns or whatever. He answered by saying he 'made money' – by going for any profitable market opportunity he could identify and satisfy, be it Davy Crockett hats, hot pants, leg-warmers or SAS balaclavas. Largely, I think, because of over-specialisation in management, this kind of thinking is now seemingly too abstract for most salaried managers. Perhaps because it is not expected of them. Top management in established businesses tends to look for people to perform adequately within tightly defined systems, budgets and mini profit centres. This makes for ease of competent cascade-style management from the top. It expects relatively little from the production, finance, marketing, personnel and other managers than to administer the systems ordained for them – management by exception with autonomy tightly defined. Line management in effect can then resemble trained alsatians, barking and wagging their tails to agreed corporate cues.

The specialisation of management and the sophistication of divisional and departmental control procedures has led to safe and mediocre management being preferred to operate them, at the expense of more dynamic and creative people – people who might take risks, who might think more for themselves, or who simply would be driven mad by working in corporate strait-jackets for people they don't respect. They would as a result not prove good long-term investments.

All of this is not simply a factor of size of organisation. I have seen the same things in smaller companies where top management only looked to junior and middle management to carry out plans reliably, not to question them nor contribute in any meaningful way to the firm's overall business strategy.

It is true that you can categorise people into those who think you can categorise people and those who don't . . . yet I do believe that most of us can spot these safe corporate archetypes from a mile off. At worst they have a kind of wide-eyed corporate zeal, they dress safely, are conspicuously happily married, play enough sport to mention it (rapidly assimilating whatever it is the boss does – sailing, golf, squash, whatever), they have little humour or wit and 'loved school', but have little creative or artistic flair or appreciation, and have dug a cultural moat around themselves. They show little warmth or urbanity and are – not surprisingly – awful people to sit next to at dinner parties.

They are, however, hard-working, well-trained, safe company people, safe subordinates in terms of in-company loyalties, and pay great to pedantic attention to detail. In short, they are just the men and women to employ to keep that short nose ahead – and what's wrong with that? Emulating them is probably the safest and easiest way to middle-class security. You don't have to be that bright. You just have to work hard and sublimate a certain amount of your individuality – an achievable goal for almost anyone who wants it enough.

No apologies for the cynicism. Knowing yourself can be painful. For most of us getting on is not about being brilliant, it is about marketing – offering what you know your bosses or your customers think they want. There is little to gain, and even something to lose, by trying to be better than is needed to do the job. Value engineering comes to human engineering.

In his book *Human Engineering*\*, Lord Robens – a man with unique experience of government, the public and private sectors, of trade unions, boardrooms and business academia – talks about the textile genius Richard Arkwright, and employers' expectations, in the past and today. Born in Bolton in 1732, Arkwright, the thirteenth child of poor parents, gave up his job as a barber at the age of thirty-five to invent and perfect a spinning frame powered by water. He became the richest cotton spinner in England and died with a fortune of half a million pounds. But, says Robens, a modern industrial organisation probably could not digest a new Arkwright. If such a man were recruited as a workman he would quickly be picked out as a trouble-maker; if he joined as a management trainee he would be even more rapidly identified as someone who 'won't fit in'.

Knowing what employers want used to be a lot easier. You would have little difficulty in knowing how best to present yourself as a clerical worker at this counting house at Lichfield back in 1852. Here is an extract from the 'Office Staff Practice' rules to which you would have to adhere:

1. Godliness, cleanliness, and punctuality are the necessities of a good business.

2. This firm has reduced the hours of work and the clerical staff will now only have to be present between the hours of 7.00am and 6.00pm on weekdays.

3. Daily prayers will be held each morning in the main office. The clerical staff will be present.

4. Clothing must be of a sober nature. The clerical staff will not disport themselves in raiment of bright colours, nor will they wear hose, unless in good repair.

5. Overshoes and top-coats may not be worn in the office, but neckscarves and headwear may be worn in inclement weather.

6. A stove is provided for the benefit of clerical staff; coal and wood must be kept in the locker. It is recommended that each member of the clerical staff bring four pounds of coal each day during cold weather.

7. No member of the clerical staff may leave the room without permission from Mr Rogers. The calls of nature are permitted, and clerical staff may

\*Jonathan Cape, London, 1970

use the garden below the second gate. This area must be kept in good order.

8. No talking is allowed during business hours.

9. The craving of tobacco, wines or spirits is a human weakness, and, as such, is forbidden to all members of the clerical staff.

10. Now that the hours of business have been drastically reduced the partaking of food is allowed between 11.30am and noon, but work will not, on any account, cease.

11. Members of the clerical staff will provide their own pens. A new sharpener is available, on application to Mr Rogers.

12. Mr Rogers will nominate a senior clerk to be responsible for the cleanliness of the main office and the private office, and all boys and juniors will report to him 40 minutes before prayers, and will remain after closing hours for similar work. Brushes, brooms, scrubbers and soap are provided by the owners.

13. The new increased weekly wages are as detailed hereunder:

| Junior boys (to 11 years) | – 1/4d | Boys (to 14 years) | – 2/1d |
|---|---|---|---|
| Juniors | – 4/8d | Junior clerks | – 8/7d |
| Clerks | – 10/9d | Senior clerks (after 15 years with the owners) | – 21/-d |

The owners recognise the generosity of the new Labour Laws, but will expect a great rise in output of work to compensate for these near-Utopian conditions.

Just think, keep your head down and in fifteen years you could get Mr Rogers' job – pen sharpener and all. In fact of course, then as now, emulating Mr Rogers is the best advice possible, burying as much of your real personality as you can bear. As Francis Bacon wrote, 'anger makes dull men witty, but keeps them poor'.

So, know yourself. Are you a Richard Arkwright (few of us are), or a Mr Rogers, one of those faithful trained corporate alsatians? Are you a whizz kid or perhaps more a disillusioned, burned-out past-tense 'was-kid' hanging on in there? It is important to know, to be honest with yourself, because you need to realise what is expected of you and what you can give.

You can pay an occupational psychologist in Harley Street or elsewhere to conduct an analysis of your strengths and weaknesses. This will probe your skills and motivations, and will give a candid and generally helpful picture of yourself, and the direction your career might best take. An increasing number of companies are putting candidates for even line management jobs through tests such as these. The cost of square pegs in round holes is far higher than the consultancy fee.

One of the leading organisations in this field is the PA Consulting Group, whose Personnel Services Department have a Psychometrics Unit. They will conduct what they call a Kostick PAPI – a perception and preference inventory – which looks at various important aspects of a person's occupational skills such as leadership and temperament.

In the USA psychoanalysis is widely used by businessmen and women to ease stress and help with setting attainable personal goals. This is likely to grow in the UK. Already Berne's transactional analysis approach is as common a subject on business school courses as discounted cash flow, and Anglo Saxon prejudices against psychiatry and psychology are falling slowly but perceptibly away. Sir Michael Edwardes in his days at British Leyland made extensive use of psychological testing to evaluate the intellectual capacity, style and approach of his senior executives. This began with executive directors, then went on to include the top 300 people and eventually some 2,000 managers.

You will not improve until you really have made an effort to know yourself – at least as well as a current or potential employer might. There follow two assessment analyses especially drawn up for this book by research psychologist Dr David Lewis. The first will tell you about your management styles, your strengths and weaknesses, and the second is a teamwork analysis which will show what you are like to work with. Fill them in now. They are fun and revealing. They will also immediately throw up a real pointer to your self-assertion – whether or not you can overcome a lifetime's prejudice about writing on a book.

**Assessment tables begin on the following page.**

## In Pursuit of Mediocrity?

It is a common mistake made by most of us in domestic and business life to compare ourselves with conspicuously successful people who we admire and would love to be like.

Socially I envy the charm and charisma of great raconteurs like the late David Niven or Peter Ustinov, and I wish I looked as good as 007 in a dinner jacket, could drive off a tee like Ballesteros and was as sickeningly good at just about everything as Dudley Moore. Realistically, of course, I adjust my sights – I have half a dozen reliable after-dinner stories up my sleeve which seem to work well enough; I may feel more like a waiter than James Bond but in a dark corner of the Dorchester I look OK in my consommé-stained tux; I occasionally slice my hook to produce a straight drive down the fairway; and I can casually rattle off the odd Cole Porter and finish before anyone notices I never touch a black note on the keyboard. It isn't great, but it's generally enough.

Why then do we still feel the need to aspire to superstar status in our business lives? The success of the rash of best-selling 'look at me, Ma' books over recent years from tycoons and consultants suggests to me that people have been less interested in them as kinds of biographies, and more interested in learning from them to emulate their success. This is I think self-evidently dangerous. By sporting analogy definition

(*text continued page 24*)

Complete this assessment by noting the response which best reflects your feelings about the statements. Ring your responses to each of the thirty questions or — if you really must. — list them *alongside the question number* on a separate sheet of paper (you are going to have to do more than simply add up all the (a), (b), (c) and (d)s). It is important to answer honestly in order to gain an accurate insight into your real approach to business.

**1  I am skilled at getting my own way.**
(a) Very true (b) True much of the time (c) Occasionally true (d) Hardly true at all.

**2  I achieve my goals in life.**
(a) Very true (b) True much of the time (c) Occasionally true (d) Hardly ever true.

**3  I demand recognition for my accomplishments.**
(a) Very true (b) True much of the time (c) Occasionally true (d) Not true at all.

**4  I pride myself on offering moral leadership.**
(a) Very true (b) True much of the time (c) Occasionally true (d) Not true at all.

**5  I believe most problems in life are best left to solve themselves.**
(a) Very true (b) True much of the time (c) Occasionally true (d) Not true at all.

**6  I face the future with great optimism.**
(a) Very true (b) True much of the time (c) Occasionally true (d) Not true at all.

**7  I take advantage of other people's weaknesses.**
(a) Very true (b) True much of the time (c) Occasionally true (d) Not true at all.

**8  I manipulate situations to suit my own purposes.**
(a) Very true (b) True much of the time (c) Occasionally true (d) Not true at all.

**9  I offer sound advice.**
(a) Very true (b) True much of the time (c) Occasionally true (d) Hardly ever true.

**10  I set myself tough challenges in life.**
(a) Very true (b) True much of the time (c) Occasionally true (d) Not true at all.

**11  I believe most people have a lot of good in them.**
(a) Very true (b) True much of the time (c) Occasionally true (d) Not true at all.

**12  I am cautious about adopting new ideas.**
(a) Very true (b) True much of the time (c) Occasionally true (d) Not true at all.

**13  I get a thrill out of being in the public eye.**
(a) Very true (b) True much of the time (c) Occasionally true (d) Not true at all.

**14  I am an excellent judge of people.**
(a) Very true (b) True much of the time (c) Occasionally true (d) Not true at all.

**15  I will be ruthless, if necessary, to achieve my goals in life.**
(a) Very true (b) True much of the time (c) Occasionally true (d) Not true at all.

**16  I trust my colleagues absolutely.**
(a) Very true (b) True to a considerable extent (c) True to some extent (d) Not true at all.

**17  I make detailed plans for the future.**
(a) Very true (b) True to a considerable extent (c) True to some extent (d) Not true at all.

**18  I love being in front of an audience.**
(a) Very true (b) True to a considerable extent (c) True to some extent (d) Not true at all.

**19  I take pride in working longer hours than most of my colleagues.**
(a) Very true (b) True much of the time (c) Occasionally true (d) Not true at all.

**20  I am wise in the ways of the world.**
(a) Very true (b) True to a considerable extent (c) True to some extent (d) Not true at all.

**21  I like to know everything that goes on at work.**
(a) Very true (b) True much of the time (c) Occasionally true (d) Hardly ever true.

**22  I avoid taking risks.**
(a) Very true (b) True much of the time (c) Occasionally true (d) Hardly ever true.

**23  I am reluctant to introduce changes at work.**
(a) Very true (b) True to a considerable extent (c) True to some extent (d) Not true at all.

**24  I don't like to think about my failures.**
(a) Very true (b) True much of the time (c) Occasionally true (d) Hardly ever true.

**25  I seek ways of making myself more popular.**
(a) Very true (b) True much of the time (c) Occasionally true (d) Hardly ever true.

**26  I am always ready to offer advice.**
(a) Very true (b) True much of the time (c) Occasionally true (d) Hardly ever true.

**27  I thrive on hard work.**
(a) Very true (b) True much of the time (c) Occasionally true (d) Hardly ever true.

**28  I constantly strive for perfection.**
(a) Very true (b) True much of the time (c) Occasionally true (d) Not true at all.

**29  I believe every cloud has a silver lining.**
(a) Very true (b) True much of the time (c) Occasionally true (d) Hardly ever true.

**30  I have a very charismatic personality.**
(a) Very true (b) True much of the time (c) Occasionally true (d) Not true at all.

## How to score

The assessment has explored six management styles. Score by awarding four points for each (a) response, two for (b), one for (c) and zero for (d), according to the table below. For example, if your answer to question one was (b), write (b) alongside the Machiavelli line under 'Your Scores'. If your answer to question two was (a), write (a) alongside the Superman line, and so on. Then add up the score for each 'Management Style' line and enter it under 'Totals'.

| Management Style | Statements | Your Scores | Totals |
|---|---|---|---|
| Machiavelli | 1; 7; 8; 15; 21 | | |
| Panglossian | 6; 11; 16; 24; 29 | | |
| Superman | 2; 10; 19; 27; 28 | | |
| Starquest | 3; 13; 18; 25; 30 | | |
| Noah | 5; 12; 17; 22; 23 | | |
| Guru | 4; 9; 14; 20; 26 | | |

To see how these styles relate to one another and the extent to which they may prove a help or a handicap in your career, fill in your scores on the table opposite by drawing them in as a bar chart. Simply rule off each score in the six columns and sketch in some diagonal lines under each line to fill it in.

## What your scores reveal

The highest score represents your primary management style, the second highest your next most frequently adopted approach. Similar scores on two or more styles means you are able to switch between them according to circumstances.

Ideally all the qualities explored by this assessment, and described below, should be present for effective management and should rate around ten. However, if any of the scores is higher than ten, there is a real risk of it dominating your strategic thinking to the point where it becomes inflexible and far less effective. Scores below ten, however, suggest that the style is used too infrequently, so reducing your effectiveness in many situations. The higher or lower the score the less successfully you are employing that particular style.

Practise using those on which your score was low, and try to reduce the frequency of high-scoring approaches.

## What the styles involve

**Machiavelli** was the celebrated Florentine statesman and author of *The Prince*, a classic account of ruthless statecraft.

As a result his name has long been synonymous with intrigue and low cunning. In moderation this can be a valuable management skill, allowing you to out think and out manoeuvre the opposition. It can help you pre-empt the intrigues of others, and proves an invaluable survival skill at times of boardroom coups. When the game is hard, fast and dirty, the competition tough and no prisoners are being taken, a Machiavelli style really comes into its own. Taken to extremes, however, it poisons the atmosphere by breeding widespread mistrust and undermining morale.

**Pangloss** was a character in Voltaire's *Candide* renowned for his incurable and

# Management Style Profile

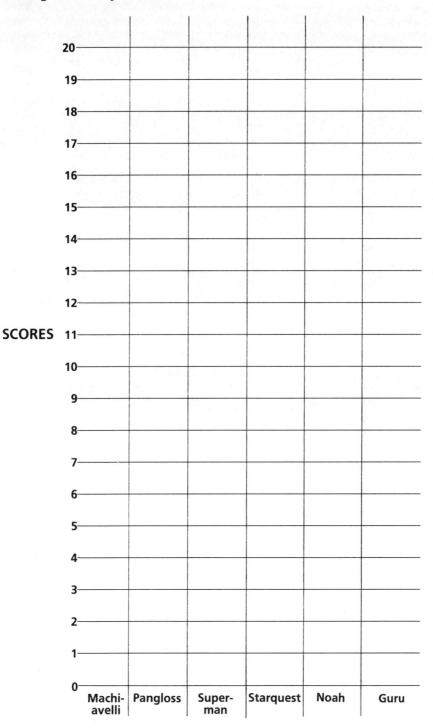

SCORES

|   | Machiavelli | Pangloss | Superman | Starquest | Noah | Guru |
|---|---|---|---|---|---|---|

20 · 19 · 18 · 17 · 16 · 15 · 14 · 13 · 12 · 11 · 10 · 9 · 8 · 7 · 6 · 5 · 4 · 3 · 2 · 1 · 0

misleading optimism. Despite the misfortunes it brought him, he believed to the end that 'all is for the best in this best of all possible worlds'. While it's always better to look on the bright side than to wallow in every misfortune, excessive optimism is as ineffective a management style as complete pessimism. A balance must be struck in order to confront problems objectively, and anticipate when, where and why things may go awry.

**Superman:** there needs to be more than a touch of superman in every successful executive. If you don't have great faith in your abilities, who else will? But some executives get so carried away by a belief in their superhuman abilities they mistrust any judgement but their own, refuse to delegate and are prime candidates for coronary heart disease. Overdoing the macho approach risks destroying all you have strived so hard to create.

**Starquest:** when this style dominates there is a constant desire to win the admiration, approval and – above all – the attention of others.
   Playing to the gallery and yearning for applause means that decisions are too often influenced by the glory they are likely to attract, instead of sound management practice. Those who always need to be centre stage are hard to work for and almost impossible to work with. While it's important to ensure one's accomplishments are noticed, this doesn't mean constantly stealing the limelight. The place for stars is show business, not big business.

**Noah:** he paid attention to warnings from a reliable source, prudently built his ark and so weathered a storm. And it's true that the ark was built by amateurs and the *Titanic* by professionals. There are certainly times when Noah's cautious, DIY play-safe style is no more than sound common sense and good business practice. But, these days, running for shelter whenever economic storms are threatened or the going gets rough means you spend more time battening down the hatches than building up the business.
   Some managers are so concerned never to get their feet wet that every decision is influenced by fears of a flood which never arrives. While a certain amount of prudence is essential, when taken to extremes it lands you high and dry in a desert of missed chances, and lost opportunities.

**Guru:** a high score here suggests you may too often set yourself up as the office guru or know-all. If so, beware, because outside your special area of expertise your views may be no better than those of anybody else – and are almost certainly inferior to those with specialist training in their field. Guru style can be a spin-off from the superman syndrome, the conviction that the possession of superior wisdom and knowledge entitles one to give advice and pass judgement on every issue. Insisting always that others hear, or worse yet, act on your generalised non-specialist views not only creates justifiable resentment, but also increases the risk of major errors.

Effective teamwork means balancing decision-making styles. This assessment will allow you to identify your own style, and discover its strengths and weaknesses. Answer the following questions by selecting your most likely response to the situation described.

**1  You are given three hot tips at the race track. The first two romp home and you win £1,000. Will you . . .**
(a) Risk all you've won on the last horse tipped, which is running at odds of 10:1?
(b) Decide your luck can't hold out any longer and go home with your winnings?
(c) Put half your winnings on the last horse, so that you won't go home empty-handed if it does let you down?

**2  You have to move quickly to another part of the country and put your house on the market. The following day you receive a cash offer, but at £5,000 less than your asking price. The purchaser insists that this is his top price.**

**The offer is well below your property's true value and acceptance will put you out of pocket on the new purchase. But you also know there is a serious downturn in house sales in your part of the country and properties similar in price and features to your own are unsold after more than a year. If this happens to you the interest on a large bridging loan will amount to more than you will lose by taking the first offer. Will you . . .**
(a) Turn the offer down flat in the hope of getting your asking price?
(b) Accept rather than lose a rapid sale?
(c) Stall for as long as possible to keep the prospective purchaser interested while you seek a better offer?

**3  You were foolish enough to lend a friend £5,000. Now he says his business has failed, he has few assets and cannot repay the loan. But he makes you an offer. He will either give you his last remaining cash, amounting to £2,500, or offer a wager on the toss of a coin.**

**If he wins you cancel the debt. If he loses, his wife has agreed to part with a family heirloom, a diamond necklace worth £10,000. Do you . . .**
(a) Take the bet because you stand a 50/50 chance of doubling your money?
(b) Settle for the £2,500?
(c) Reject both proposals and insist he find another way of settling his debt in full?

**4  While on a business trip abroad you contract a painful and distressing but non-fatal virus. The doctors you consult say there is no cure. Then you find one who has supplies of an experimental drug. He warns that while it has cured similar cases there have also been some fatalities which might have been due to the drug, although this has not been proved. He has only a small amount left, no chance of getting any more and another patient in similar circumstances may claim it before you. Do you . . .**
(a) Agree to the treatment immediately so as not to miss what might be your only chance of a cure?
(b) Turn it down and continue to search for a safe cure?
(c) Risk a 48 hour delay before making your decision, so as to try and obtain a second opinion about the risks involved?

**5** You have decided to invest some of your hard-earned savings on the stock market. Three companies are of interest to you.

The first is a solid but unexciting blue chip stock that will return a steady dividend but never make your fortune.

The second is a small mining company which, you have heard a whisper, is about to announce a big strike. If true their stocks will soar and you'll reap big rewards. If false their shares will probably prove worthless.

Finally there is a manufacturing firm which, it is rumoured, will soon be taken over. Should the take-over occur you'll have made an excellent investment. But even without any change it should return a modest profit, but one less than the blue chip company. Are you most likely to . . .

(a) Take a big gamble with the mining company?
(b) Play safe with a blue chip investment?
(c) Decide on shares in the manufacturing firm?

**6** Your son is about to start studying law at a prestige university. The trouble is he is far more interested in music than a legal career. He has played lead guitar in an amateur group for many years and musician friends assure you he is very gifted, and the group extremely talented. A week before his studies are due to begin, the group get the offer of an American tour.

If he accepts it could be the first step to wealth and fame, but he'll lose his place at law school. If he turns down the offer the group will lose what might be the chance of a lifetime. He asks your advice. Do you . . .

(a) Tell him to take the chance in music, after all there are other law schools if the group flops?
(b) Urge him to forget the tour and not lose the opportunity of obtaining such a prestigious degree?
(c) Suggest that he try to obtain a deferment from the law school so that he can go on the tour without risking his place?

**7** An American business associate dines at your house and admires a bronze statue in the lounge. You paid £5 for it in a junk shop and loathe it. He says it would be perfect for his home in Texas and offers £500 in cash. You suspect that, while his liking for the bronze could be genuine, he might also know that it is worth far more. Do you . . .

(a) Refuse his offer on the chance that you'll make more by selling at auction?
(b) Accept since you'll have made an excellent profit on something you dislike and may not even be worth £500?
(c) Insist on a valuation before agreeing, even though this could put the sale at risk?

To score this assessment simply total up the number of (a)s, (b)s and (c)s selected.

## Majority of (a)s

This is the decision-making style of a *maximiser*. You are willing to take big risks in the hope of maximum rewards. You approach challenges with optimism and confidence, always certain you'll come out on top.

**Strengths.** Sensitivity to the positive aspects of any course of action means that opportunities not obvious to less optimistic decision-makers will be quickly seen. This style typifies the entrepreneur. Teams need somebody who can think big and not shy away from risks.

**Weaknesses.** The willingness to 'go for broke' on every occasion means big wins can be wiped out by equally spectacular losses.

Maximisers on teams need to be balanced by the far more cautious approach of those with a majority of (b)s.

## Majority of (b)s

This indicates a *minimising* decision-making style. You always seek to minimise losses should, as you pessimistically predict, things go badly wrong.
**Strengths.** This style is ideally suited to situations entailing a high risk of material loss, whether money or goods. Minimisers are excellent at managing other people's finances because they are unlikely to take risks on speculative proposals, however tempting.
**Weaknesses.** Excessive caution may lead to lost opportunities and missed chances. A team dominated by minimisers will seldom make a mistake – or anything else.

The exact opposite of the maximiser approach, conflict can arise in a team where these two are opposed. But from such a clash can come sound decisions in which neither lose out on opportunities nor involve the company in excessive risks.

## Majority of (c)s

This is the style of a *minimaxer* whose decisions are strongly influenced by the desire to both minimise their maximum potential loss and maximise their minimum expected gain in any situation.
**Strengths.** Unlike the maximiser who sees only the chance for a big success or the minimiser who emphasises the risks of disaster, the minimaxer pursues a middle course. He, or she, is very aware of discrepancies between what was actually achieved and what might have been accomplished. Minimaxers are irritated by lost chances and powerfully desire to prevent later regrets.

It is a style that comes into its own whenever a team is faced with having to take a decision without knowing enough about the situation.
**Weaknesses.** Because the minimaxer tends to favour a compromise between two extremes, he, or she, is as unlikely to enjoy spectacular coups as to experience catastrophic failures.

If you scored near equal totals on all three letters then you have a very flexible decision-making style and can adapt well to different situations.

To be successful, a team should combine all three styles in equal amounts under a strong but empathic and objective chairperson, who keeps lines of communications open between all team members and has the courage to support both the risk-taking of the maximiser and the caution of the minimiser as the situation requires.

'winners' will always be in a tiny minority and if we invite comparison between the few and ourselves, we will inevitably begin to view ourselves as 'losers', which for the most part the majority of us are not.

Instead I believe we should learn to know and understand the rather peculiar nature of the motivations and chemistry of tycoons and 'winners' before we even consider emulating them or envying them. These conspicuous business superstars are in themselves highly untypical of top management, and the route to the top of our own aspirational tree is probably much easier than these managerial commando types would have us think.

It is clear to me that most British companies are driven by a desire from the top for survival and safe success. The reason for the business beginning – the identification by the founders of an opportunity to supply some product or service to customers at a healthy profit – has been lost in a sea of systems, budgets and meetings, to the point that these tools of management have become an end in themselves. The inertia within organisations simply to exist and carry on doing things they have always done can be very strong, and become a kind of unwritten but sacred business objective in itself.

If you had asked the founders and original venture capitalists of most now well-established firms if they would have risked money, time and reputations to earn more or less what they could get with money on deposit or in blue chip investments, they would have thought you mad. The real pre-tax rate of return for industrial and commercial companies in the UK, when North Sea activities are excluded, averaged six per cent for the decade to the mid-1980s, and was as low as three per cent in the early 1970s.

Granny with her tax-free government savings has barely done any worse.

It begs the question of why so many 'safe' businesses bother to carry on at all. If their owners *could* capitalise, they could do almost as well, with less risk, in any number of other investments. In so many firms that original spark, the eye for the main chance, has been lost or forgotten. Why is this?

When you talk to receivers about what causes most established businesses to fail they will give you many reasons – cash flow problems, over-trading, poor marketing and the rest. A common thread running through a great many, however, is that of clogs-to-clogs in two, or perhaps clogs-to-Gucci-loafers-to-clogs in three generations. Second or third generation owners of businesses often lack the drive or interest to keep the firm thrusting ahead, and frequently do not see the need to find somebody else who can before a debenture holder – normally the bank – calls in a receiver. The same thing can happen with the first generation entrepreneur, too, especially where they have perhaps diversified into other new and more challenging ventures or have capitalised handsomely.

Each year there are more than 20,000 liquidations and bankruptcies in the UK. Only one new business start-up in ten will still be around after five years, and after ten years only one in one hundred will still be operating successfully. Some 700 directors each year are made personally bankrupt, and many more than this lose all or almost all their assets and homes when their companies fold – mostly as a result of their having given personal guarantees. These figures are only the tip of the iceberg. Many thousands of other company directors, sole traders and partnerships come to the end of the line and reluctantly close down or wind down their businesses, just as many thousands of men and women overreach themselves in their personal lives through heavy mortgage or other credit commitments. Most new business ventures fail, most new product launches fail, most people who suddenly try to be what they are not fail. Doctors may bury their mistakes, lawyers send theirs to jail. Businessmen and women however have nowhere to hide when things go wrong.

It is one of the harsh realities of life that dreamers have to accept. The successful entrepreneur is a rare and generally fairly obnoxious animal. Think hard before you aspire to become one yourself. The shops that spring up in small town High Streets selling stuffed toys, hand-crafted goods and the like, all with clever sounding names – long agonised over – with beautiful stationery, are truly heart-rending. You see their fresh-faced proprietors in there for the first few weeks, rearranging their lovely window displays. But nobody goes in – and if they do they spend little. The shops are always empty. Their owners put on a brave face and still turn out to open to nobody at 9.30 each morning, six days a week, until the dream bursts. The true entrepreneur would never have been in that business and even if he or she had they would have imported from Taiwan and supplied big department stores. The true entrepreneur would have had his offices off the expensive High Street in an old warehouse or over a shoe shop. They would not have agonised over a name; they would have bought a shelf name of an existing company and gone with that – it's cheaper and quicker.

Most people are not cut out to start businesses, to go in and turn problem companies around or to live like Martini people. Their main burning drives in life are generally procreational or recreational. They want job satisfaction, peer group status and a competitive remuneration package, but probably get much less *real* satisfaction from the fruit of their labours than from the fruit of their loins, or from the end of a fishing rod or number seven iron.

In the same way, most businesses are not being run with the objectives of aggressive and persistent growth and profit performance. Keeping a short nose ahead of last year's figures, the industry averages and City expectations is what most aim for, and achieve sufficiently often to retain the momentum.

Assessment Three has been drawn up to probe your perceptions of

Organisations, like individuals, have unique personalities. Sometimes this is stamped on them by a charismatic founder or MD, on other occasions it arises from the traditions, attitudes and assumptions of the company culture.

For the best chances of achievement and fulfilment your own personality should not be too far out of line with the corporate character. Test how well you and your organisation are matched by creating personality profiles for both.

All you have to do is rate first yourself, and then your organisation, on the sixteen qualities listed below.

If you imagine that those qualities which characterise your corporation were embodied in a single individual, you should have no difficulty in scoring the assessment. Place a cross at a point on the dotted line (there are ten dots in all) which reflects the extent to which you or the company possess a particular attribute. You'll find it less confusing to use different colours for the two sets of assessments.

**I am . . .**
**My company is . . .**

| | | | | | | | | | | |
|---|---|---|---|---|---|---|---|---|---|---|
| **Conservative** | . | . | . | . | . | . | . | . | . | **Radical** |
| **Tough-minded** | . | . | . | . | . | . | . | . | . | **Tender-hearted** |
| **Perfectionist** | . | . | . | . | . | . | . | . | . | **Casual** |
| **Orthodox** | . | . | . | . | . | . | . | . | . | **Unorthodox** |
| **Thrusting** | . | . | . | . | . | . | . | . | . | **Diffident** |
| **Confident** | . | . | . | . | . | . | . | . | . | **Uncertain** |
| **Determined** | . | . | . | . | . | . | . | . | . | **Hesitant** |
| **Painstaking** | . | . | . | . | . | . | . | . | . | **Slapdash** |
| **Predatory** | . | . | . | . | . | . | . | . | . | **Passive** |
| **Traditional** | . | . | . | . | . | . | . | . | . | **Innovative** |
| **Inflexible** | . | . | . | . | . | . | . | . | . | **Flexible** |
| **Practical** | . | . | . | . | . | . | . | . | . | **Impractical** |
| **Go ahead** | . | . | . | . | . | . | . | . | . | **Hidebound** |
| **Responsible** | . | . | . | . | . | . | . | . | . | **Irresponsible** |
| **Moral** | . | . | . | . | . | . | . | . | . | **Unethical** |
| **Energetic** | . | . | . | . | . | . | . | . | . | **Lethargic** |

Connect the dots to create the two profiles. Notice where they correspond and differ. If there are significant mismatches between the two, ask yourself how important those attributes on which you diverge are to you. Major differences in attitude or approach can produce frustration, anxiety and depression. If you and your organisation are mismatched either you must change (the most likely unless you are the new boss), or there should be more give and take from each.

your own organisation. It will help you think through just what the *real* corporate, divisional or departmental goals are so far as they influence your own role within them. Filling it in will tell you more about yourself and your real view about the organisation than it would tell an outsider about the organisation itself. Office and corporate politics are real enough. Just as real as court politics, and there have been enough heads rotting on pikes off Tower Bridge to testify to that. It is, however, the second important step in the business of knowing yourself – knowing your organisation, and what it wants from you.

## A Safe Future?

If you are an average person working for an average organisation then the comfortable message that safe mediocrity has so far been enough will have been reassuring, if cynical. This book is not primarily about whether this is right or wrong, and it is not an evangelistic book designed to point average people and companies towards the pursuit of excellence. It is rather about how individuals and organisations can best achieve their own agreed objectives, be they modest or thrusting.

There is nothing but frustration facing an executive trying to change the world in a company culture set by a board that believes their world is perfectly alright as it is, thank you. There is nothing to gain, and possibly much to lose, if the chief executive of a perfectly successful manufacturing business suddenly starts acting like some demented Japanese/ Pacific Basin born-again capitalist.

The good news is that you do not have to be Richard Arkwright to do very nicely in your career, and as a company you do not have to invent cat's eyes, photocopying technology and microwave cookers every year to stay in the game. What is expected from you by your boss, your customers, shareholders and employees alike is generally quite modest and attainable. The key is to find out just what it is they think they want from you, and to present it to them – bring them into your world.

The bad news is that whilst safe mediocrity will continue to do in some soft markets – where margins are high to OK and competition low, thanks to protected markets, the high cost of entry, quasi-monopoly, patent protection or whatever – the increasing number of hard markets means the survival of the fittest. Hard markets include those in structural decline and those where margins and unique selling points have been savaged by domestic and international competition. De-manning, de-stocking, new technology, retail range rationalisation and the other irreversible changes mean that many people and their companies are facing harsh market realities for the first time. They are having to analyse their strengths and market with all the vigour of their founders. They have to change, and be seen to change by customers and the City alike, and that change needs managing.

# 2 Facial Prejudice

Most successful people are pleasant looking. Not necessarily handsome or pretty, but pleasant and comfortable to look at and be seen with. If you are well above or below average height, have crossed eyes, a problem with your complexion, halitosis and a taste in clothes that runs to greens and oranges, then you had better have something very special to bring to the party. But then you already know that from trying to develop some sort of social life for yourself, don't you?

In this respect life can be cruel. In my view, boxer Joe Bugner was the best heavyweight this country has seen in a very long time – doing well with the world's best, Ali and Frazier, as well as beating Henry Cooper in a still controversial points decision. Unlike Cooper, however, who was and remains a national hero, Bugner never really won the hearts of the British public. I think this was due in no small measure to his rather high-pitched voice, which seemed wrong for such a huge body.

Over the past ten years I have interviewed over three thousand people for executive jobs. Despite excellent paper qualifications and experience, some just physically grated on me from the first few seconds of the meeting. I use the five-point plan for grading applicants – scoring marks out of ten in the categories: first impressions, qualifications, background, motivations and aptitude. In practice the first impressions mark can be all that matters, because if the first look to me seems wrong, then it will to my customers/clients.

The great danger is that you find yourself only employing the kind of people you would enjoy having round to dinner. To avoid this 'bring on the clones' risk, some years ago I took on someone who did jar with me, but who seemed perfect in every other respect. A bit of grit in the oyster, I thought. Brave stuff. In fact it proved to be a mistake and I have not risked flying in the face of first impressions since. If I were recruiting neuro-surgeons or experts in long chain molecules, then the weighting in my five-point plan might be different, but most of us are relative generalists in highly competitive job markets and first impressions remain crucial.

I don't feel too guilty about perhaps jumping to conclusions about interviewees based on their appearance and attractiveness. Research by Dr Walter Berger (with Heinz Schuler) of the University of Ausburg, Germany, showed that eighty personnel managers behaved in much the same way. Faked job application forms with photographs of a range of people were sent to the personnel specialists. The results showed that the more attractive applicants in the photographs stood a much better chance of being asked in for an interview, and that they were thought likely to be more friendly, more creative and more highly motivated than the rest.

Maturity is another factor which can influence interviewers. Amongst graduates, I have always found the women a good three to four years ahead of their male colleagues in this respect. Nine out of ten graduates my company took on were women, largely for this reason. Subsequent work experience invariably proved first impressions to be correct.

At the other extreme, men over-mature in years do seem to try too hard, instead of using their grey hairs as an asset. A section from one of the short stories in Truman Capote's *Music for Chameleons** haunts me as I launch into middle age. His character, suddenly feeling old at fifty-two, describes the old days when girls found him attractive. 'I always had such confidence. Just walking down the street, I felt such a *swing*. I could feel people looking at me – on the street, in a restaurant, at a party . . .' Now he seems to have become the invisible man . . . and the pretty girls at a recent party just saw him as 'a tired old guy who smiled too much'. Brilliant writing, and a sharp lesson for us all.

Physical appearance, as we shall see, is a form of membership card to group acceptance. The importance of belonging to a group, the tribal spirit, is clear enough in the business world as in so many other areas of life as a whole where we badge ourselves, with political opinions, musical tastes, car marques, newspapers or whatever. We *do* want to be a member of a club that would let us join, despite Marxist theory to the contrary (Groucho, that is). So with people. All the research shows we generally warm to people like us and dislike people not like us.

This can be based on territorial tribalism, something that has led to non-psycopaths committing appalling acts of violence in wartime upon people they have been able to downgrade in their minds as lesser humans.

The deliberate use of territorial rights and the dark and dangerous emotions they can arouse has become a popular management device. I distrust and dislike the creation and use of groups in this way within companies. It is everything successful management should not be about in my opinion. Competition with the company's own past performance, and with competitors in the market place, can inculcate only positive drives and help generate the feeling of belonging to a worthwhile whole. Competition between production lines, between other departments or between other divisions in the same group, seems to me to be on the whole a mistake. It can lead to short-term benefits in terms of productivity and identification with achievable objectives, and it is managerially very attractive and tidy. Dividing to conquer also becomes easier if that is what is wanted. The trained alsatians can run a system like this very well. But management systems are not there to be tidy and easy – they are there to be effective, and to get the best out of people over the medium to long term.

*Hamish Hamilton, London, 1981

What the 'group' debate highlights is the different approach adopted by organisations to their people. Put as an extreme, some companies are run based on the concept that compartmentalised teamwork is the answer, others that corporate teamwork, maximising the contribution of individuals, is more effective.

The seeds of the group approach were innocent enough. They grew from work of Professor Elton Mayo, and followed some early investigations into the social aspects of working life in the late 1920s/early 1930s at the Hawthorne plant of the General Electric Company in Chicago. These showed the importance of the immediate work group and social acceptance within it to employees, and led to humanistic psychology – the 'Group Dynamic', sensitivity training and 'T-Group' sessions which became so popular, especially during the 1960s. Everyone at the time knew stories of fully grown men and women, as managers, openly weeping at T-Groups (Training Groups) because of their seeming inability to win acceptance or to assert their leadership amongst a hostile cabal. I have no doubt that many of these psychological wounds never healed. The basic theory was that if workers are more open and trusting with each other, they would become more productive; the group would tend to know best. But this can perversely snuff out individualism and initiative outside arbitrarily set boundaries. On the positive side, the plan was to break down basically autocratic management structures into groups of small, democratic teams. Individuals within the T-Groups would hopefully be more receptive to the views of others around them, more tactful and tolerant and less likely to make instant judgements on their own. Some estimates suggest, however, that only up to 40 per cent of people put through T-Groups improved their inter-personal skills, and then for how long?

*The Organisation Man*, a hard-hitting management book by William H. Whyte Jnr, published in 1955, begged to differ and there has since been a steady swing back toward the centre – using groups successfully for briefing purposes in a cascade management system, but looking for corporate commitment, and the maximisation of individual potential by more and better training and by formalised appraisal systems.

Tribal we remain however. That will not change. It is important to know whether in your organisation you are expected to tread the big tribal stage in a corporate sense, or whether your performance and potential is still being measured against the smaller, departmental group structure. What is expected of you will differ, and what you offer and the way you offer it may have to change.

## Physical Appearance

Any barrister will tell you that juries can be heavily influenced by how a defendant looks and presents his or herself. In the USA there has been extensive research into this subject by Harry Kalven and Hans Zeisel of

Chicago University. One case reported concerned a man charged with raping his daughter, aged ten. He was found guilty and given a life sentence. On appeal the jury came up with a hung verdict at the re-trial. Then, at the third trial, the jury declared a 'not guilty' verdict, and even gave the man sixty-eight dollars they had chipped in to show their sympathy. Presumably, come trial three, the man's ability to project himself and his side of the story had improved dramatically.

That was some time ago, but the advent of video technology has today been seized upon by many lawyers in the USA to coach witnesses to present themselves well. Experience also shows that having a 'criminal's face' means you are more likely to be treated like a criminal and to act like one. In Texas a small proportion of the $22 million a year spent rehabilitating offenders goes on plastic surgery, at first as a reward for good behaviour, but now directed at the most needy.

On a day to day basis, all of us are aware that some people we meet raise our hackles, and others can seem like lifelong friends after just a couple of meetings. In his book, *Contact: The First Four Minutes*\*, written with Natalie Zunin, psychiatrist Leonard Zunin suggests that four minutes is how long it takes for people to weigh each other up and decide whether or not to develop friendships. All this may seem the luck of the draw, a quirk of fate, you hit it off with some people or you don't. How far can we really alter the hand that nature may have dealt us?

## The Face

The face may be one person's fortune, but to others it can seem like their biggest liability in life.

Eye contact is the most immediate signal we give out and receive in meetings. Weighing people up is a common enough part of new encounters, but the eyes can and often do immediately establish a friendly or hostile relationship, a master or servant role. It has become common for boxers to stare fixedly at each other for the seconds before a big fight begins. Some research, pioneered by Professor Eckhard Hess when he was working at Chicago University, suggests that the extent to which the pupil of a person's eye dilates can give out positive or negative signals.

Some people firmly believe they can read faces and deduce character traits accurately. Others have firm prejudices about people with beards, with red hair or with eyes too close together. I have an irrational dislike of people whose eyebrows meet, and have long since developed the pretty disgusting habit of plucking mine in the middle with my fingernails. From childhood days all nasty people were ugly (the ugly sisters, the wicked witch etc) and all heroes and heroines were attractive white Caucasians. Religious and ethnic minorities can also point to early

*Ballantine Books, New York, 1972*

influences which have created harmful prejudices, sadly many of them in great literature – Shakespeare's Shylock, Dickens' Fagin, Defoe's servile Man Friday. In a different mood, however, Defoe made the mocking remark that there were 'a hundred thousand fellows ready to fight to the death against popery, without knowing whether popery was a man or a horse'.

There was a time when 'science' was brought to the study of the face. Jonathan Kaspar Lavater, a Swiss, developed techniques to predict a person's personality from the face, based on such measurements as the size of nose and distance between the eyes. Charles Darwin's eccentric cousin, Sir Francis Galton (he was one of the pioneers of the use of fingerprinting for identification), launched his own system for the 'measurement' of attractiveness. He believed that the physical and mental attractiveness of humans could be improved by selective mating – a science he called eugenics. Craniology had also been developed, paving the way for untold quasi-scientific racism. Sweden's Anders Retzius developed a cranial index classifying head shapes, which led to the debate about skull size, the size of brain and level of intelligence. The shape of things to come arrived in the form of Italian Cesare Lombroso, who came up with a link between skull and other physical measurements, such as a receding forehead and the propensity to commit crime. In 1876, a time when crime and immorality were more closely linked than today, he published *L'uomo delinquente* – 'The Delinquent Man' – arguing that criminals are born and have identifiable physical characteristics.

Even Beethoven did not escape some of this type of questionable science. When he died in 1827 in Vienna, the doctors conducted a post-mortem to discover, amongst other things, why his brain was so musical. His death mask was made after the post-mortem, and is less accurate as a result.

The Victorians had any number of encouragements, were any needed, to pigeon-hole people by physical appearance. In 'The Strange Case of Dr Jekyll and Mr Hyde', Robert Louis Stevenson created the archetype character whose physical presence somehow radiated evil and fear. He describes Mr Hyde as pale and dwarfish, 'he gave an impression of deformity without any nameable malformation, he had a displeasing smile . . . all these were points against him; but not all of these together could explain the hitherto unknown disgust, loathing and fear with which Mr Utterson regarded him. "There must be something else," said the perplexed gentleman. "There *is* something more, if I could find a name for it. God bless me, the man seems hardly human! Something troglodytic, shall we say? Or can it be the old story of Dr Fell? or is it the mere radiance of a foul soul . . .?"'

Interestingly, despite the many film versions where the good doctor transforms into a conspicuous monster – in the early 1940s version with Spencer Tracy and Ingrid Bergman Dr Jekyll becomes darker skinned, the jaw prognathous, the teeth splayed, the brow wider and the hair and eyebrows blacker and thicker (negroid?) – Stevenson leaves the real horror of the man as something intangible. You cannot put your finger on the reason, but you *know* you detest and fear him, just as you do some people you first meet. The Doctor Fell story to which he refers perhaps gives a clue to the idea which led to the story. It comes from a verse by Thomas Brown dating to the seventeenth century:

> *I do not love you, Dr Fell,*
> *But why I cannot tell;*
> *But this I know full well,*
> *I do not love you, Dr Fell.*

Another Stevenson description of Hyde: 'I never saw a man I so disliked, and yet I scarce know why. He must be deformed somewhere; he gives a strong feeling of deformity, although I couldn't specify the point . . .'

The preoccupation with categorising facial and racial 'types' was deep-rooted. The following is a typical Victorian approach to describing a foreign face. It was written by the famous explorer/adventurer, Sir Richard Burton, in his book *First Footsteps in East Africa*, and describes the Sumali: 'The head is rather long than round, and generally of the amiable variety, it is gracefully put on the shoulders, belongs equally to Africa and Arabia, and would be exceedingly weak but for the beauty of the brow. As far as the mouth, the face, with the exception of high cheek-bones is good; the contour of the forehead enobles it; the eyes are large and well-formed, and the upper features are frequently handsome and expressive. The jaw, however, is almost invariably prognathous and African; the broad, turned-out lips betray approximation to the Negro; and the chin projects to the detriment of the facial angle . . . The mouth is course as well as thick-lipped; the teeth rarely project as in the Negro . . .'

All this from a cultured, broadminded man. A man, by the way, who subsequently had some facial problems of his own. Hostile tribesmen attacked his party and Burton escaped with 'a javelin through both cheeks, carrying away four teeth and transfixing the palate'. It did not stop him translating such Eastern erotica as *The Kama Sutra*, *The Perfumed Garden* and *Arabian Nights* for British consumption nearly thirty years later, nor from dying in his bed of natural causes in his seventieth year. No apparent problems of facial prejudice holding back the lusty Sir Richard. After his death, incidentally, his wife burned almost all his diaries for reasons not hard to imagine.

So, what to do with your own face? In Japan, where 'face' has two meanings, there is a near epidemic amongst university students to have facial plastic surgery to improve their chances of employment. Plastic and general cosmetic surgery in the West is common enough already in the USA, and in those professions like acting, modelling and popular entertainment where facial blips seem unacceptable. That hollow-cheeked, pouty beauty of some models is created by the removal of the sixes, sevens and eights teeth which partially collapses the cheeks. Even British lady prime ministers have been known to have their front teeth straightened.

If you have a serious facial problem that is affecting you psychologically and holding you back, then talk to your doctor and decide if cosmetic surgery makes sense. In certain circumstances it can be available under the National Health Service. Your doctor can obtain a list of members of the British Association of Plastic Surgeons from the Royal College of Surgeons, 35/43 Lincolns Inn Fields, London WC2A 3PN. It lists all their members and where they practise so you can find one near to you. You should only see a surgeon, however, when your GP has written a referral letter. This makes sure you are going to a properly qualified Association member, and that on-going liaison will take place with your GP.

Surgery apart there are other cosmetic steps which may be worth considering or taking advice on. The cut of your hair – for men and women – can help broaden or lengthen your face, a beard can hide a man's 'weak' or double chin problem, a moustache can disguise a 'weak' mouth or rather full lips, and any combination of spectacles, toupees, dental work, sun tans and skin treatments may also help. Women can rely more on make-up, hair styles, and jewellery to help create the impression they want. The average looking people may scoff, but if you do not believe you look alright then things can become self-prophesying – you will lack confidence and act like a loser from those first, vital few seconds onwards.

To stack the odds most strongly in your favour you should aim to look average, ordinary. It can be a mistake for even those who are naturally handsome or pretty to look too stunning, to stand out in the crowd. Darwin talked about cryptic colouration, survival by blending in with your surroundings. All the research suggests that we like average, pleasant people – people like us, people who don't threaten. The thing to remember is that ordinariness is in fact a key component of attractiveness, and that it is the absence of distinguishing features that leads to that ordinariness/attractiveness.

If you are plain to unattractive, the task of looking ordinary should not be too daunting. The Americans have much to teach us in this respect, of making the most of what we've got. I have never met an ugly middle-class American. To them, being unattractive simply is not an option. If on the other hand you are pleasant to attractive already, do not be tempted to aim for glamour and film star looks. Don't stand out too much – it can threaten others important to you and calls for a reaction from them too early in a business or social relationship.

## Dress Sense

Much the same messages apply to dress. It can be a serious matter. An industrial tribunal in 1986, for instance, heard a young ex-bank clerk claiming unfair dismissal and sex discrimination against the Royal Bank of Scotland. He refused to wear a suit – instead he wore a grey twill jacket and trousers – and was sacked.

Dark blue and grey flannel suits, plain or pin-striped, white or pale blue shirts, a sober tie and little if any male jewellery remain the ticket to safe ordinariness. Brown or light blue suits are best left to Ronald Reagan or football managers respectively; black suits to crematorium managers. I can remember being irrationally put off one man I interviewed because he wore cream-coloured silk socks. That may tell you more about me than him, but I was the one with a job to offer. The suit should be good, but no better than that you might expect your boss or customer to wear. If you drive a Porsche, keep that to yourself too.

Avoid conspicuous designer labels and keep the Cartier tank watch or gold Rolex Oyster for the evenings, even if they are Hong Kong fakes. Ordinary people do not wear them. In fact, iron out any idiosyncracies – the pocket handkerchief, the buttonhole, the bow tie, the hat, the Sherlock Holmes tweed cape, the Dunhill lighter (you should never be the first to smoke anyway), the Gucci briefcase . . . They just might strike a discord for no apparent reason, and become a suspected clue to all kinds of peculiarities he or she may imagine you have. Never trust a man with two-tone shoes (co-respondent shoes), a dicky bow or spats used to be the rule. Suede shoes and woolly cardigans or jumpers today are also definitely for weekends only.

President Kennedy is said to have worn vests and two shirts on coldish days so he could be the only one not wearing – not needing – a topcoat, making him stand out and seem more virile than he undoubtedly was. No one ever failed to come back with an order or to get through an interview for dressing 'too safely'. Nor, incidentally, has any man or woman failed to get on for being too thin. In Britain corpulence has yet to catch on, although in Germany, France, Italy and the USA it seems fine, if not *de rigueur*, for at least some very top management to be fat ('have presence' as fatties like to think, not without some justification: some *big*, big people can have a very powerful to intimidating presence). For those on the way up, however, the lean and hungry look still has to be right. Even more so for women.

As general advice, men should keep their hair short and tidy, and on their head. There was once a marvellous parliamentary exchange in the House of Commons many years ago between the then prime minister, Harold Wilson, and the late Sir Gerald Nabarro, a flamboyant Tory MP with a huge moustache. Wilson was going on in a defence debate about the trichotomy of demands on the budget, from the army, navy and air force, when Nabarro shot up and said the word should be pronounced as *tri* not *try*-chotomy. Quick as a flash Wilson pointed out that his own pronunciation was perfectly correct, and perhaps the Honourable Member had become confused with the word trichology, the study of unwanted facial hair, a subject about which . . .

Long sideburns, beards and moustaches, should all be avoided – and in that order of priority if the werewolf in you really is that strong. Research, incidentally, has shown that women find other forms of facial hair the biggest turn-off sexually of all – that is tufts of hair growing from the ears and nose. A good barber should take care of the former, and being careless with a glass of Sambouca can painfully solve the latter.

Business dressing for women is more complex in some respects, being touched by fashion, yet the central theme of plain, simple and businesslike remains the same. Winter and autumn wear is easier – suits, high-necked blouses and other such 'sensible' clothes and accessories. Remember Darwin's cryptic colouration – blending in with your surroundings. Spring and particularly summer wear can lead to some more difficult decisions. Of course you always wear a bra and only consider opting out of stockings/tights during the hottest of hot spells. Most women can make themselves *appear* a size 12 with a bit of crea-tivity on choice of bra and looseness of fit of clothes. Sexy dressing is never 'in' – low cut, off the shoulder, backless or slit dresses are not for a working environment, nor anything too figure-hugging. Colours should be muted – blues, maroons, pastels and so on. As for make-up, if you are pale consider using a little blusher – it will make you seem more healthy.

Short women can lean on two-inch heels, and generally look better in fitted outfits, preferably waisted. Businesslike trousers can make legs look longer. Japanese fashion houses designing for the West are good at making the most of short people. Taller women can wear most things and are best carrying on as if they were not tall at all. The stoop so often seen should be avoided, even when with short men – it will be seen as patronising. It *is* OK however to be seen patronising flat shoes and pumps, thanks to the *Royal* patronage of the Princess of Wales. (Harrods, and others, have an Executive Service Suite which offers free advice and guidance on finding and choosing the right outfits.)

Your choice of dress should reflect your organisation's values, not your own. Never dress beyond your status, as we are all tempted to do socially. If you are unsure whether to wear a certain outfit to the office, don't. Dress as a BBC television newscaster might – ageless and classless, unobtrusive. That goes for hair, make-up and any jewellery too. Businesswomen, be they twenty or sixty, should aim to seem at the younger or older end of middle age respectively.

## Empathy

Hitting the back of a customer's or employer's retina and achieving the surprisingly difficult status of normality is a first important step. The next concerns an almost frighteningly bewildering mix of body language, non-verbal cues, eye contact and small talk that can be summarised as empathy. It all sounds impossibly complicated and difficult to assimilate, but so does a description of walking. Just as walking is important, so are these almost subliminal body messages. Social psychologist Michael Argyle of Oxford University, for example, has estimated that non-verbal cues are 4.3 times more effective than verbal ones.

Much has been written about body language and a great deal of research has been conducted to establish something we all know intuitively – that the posture of people we are with can and generally does tell us a lot about them.

Customs officers and police interrogators are highly skilled in reading facial and body messages. Look around you at the next meeting you attend of half a dozen or more people. Without knowing all the science you will be able to spot people who are bored, disinterested, anxious, angry, attentive and so on, simply by the way they sit or stand, hold their hands, position their upper torso, incline their head . . . Watch the bar-room bore or the drunk, leaning forward, masses of eye contact, invading your natural space, anything to hold your attention while he tells you his joke or life story. The extremes of these positions are easy enough to see. What perhaps is less well understood is the way you can use body language, when understood, to elicit a subliminal response from others. Simply by the way you use your body you can relax someone, make them anxious, hurry them up, slow them down – and make them like or dislike you. You do it already without realising it.

One of the greatest artistic performances I have experienced was David Bintley dancing *Petrushka* at Covent Garden. Dance is simply another example of body language, and in *Petrushka* words become completely redundant as the beautiful girl doll, the bullying Turk, and the sad little clown Petrushka come to life as puppets after dark when the world is sleeping.

Children themselves of course are also highly skilled at body language – in the first year or two, along with various cries, it is virtually all they have with which to communicate. Watching youngsters can be very instructive for adults as the extremes of body language are so easy to spot – anger, frustration, giddy happiness, sulkiness, shyness, submissiveness, slyness, guilt, regret . . . Our Darwinian heritage with the apes in the zoo is obvious enough, animals generally using body language extensively to communicate with others. You don't need a degree in ethology to know it's not wise to pat a dog baring its teeth at you.

One problem the British, indeed the north Europeans generally, have is their gaucheness in terms of using body language and touch. I have heard all kinds of theories why it is that, say, the British are undemonstrative in this respect. Perhaps like other nations from colder climates we are used to being well wrapped up in constricting outerwear, that on cold, misty damp mornings it's a question of head down and get on with it, tending the fields. The clipped manner of speaking, through the side of the mouth, which we still hear in some of the current generation of landed gentry may have now developed into an affectation. But it could have been born from a very real need of their hardworking forebears to be short and to the point on icy cold mornings in Scotland or Gloucestershire.

Whatever the real reasons may be, it does seem that the British are far less demonstrative in terms of body language than, say, a typical Italian or Spaniard sent in from central casting. We do our best. Returning from a Greek island package holiday I decided it was time to loosen up, and launched into an enthusiastic bout of handshaking, back-slapping, shoulder-arming and innocent hugging of anyone of either sex unlucky enough to stray into my ever-expanding territory. After a week I overheard myself being made fun of as some kind of Zorba the Freak and soon after returned chastened to my usual autistic self. Small wonder the spirit of adventure is dead.

It's the same with languages. I'm convinced that there is something distinctly un-British and highly suspicious (and a bit fay) about anyone who can speak French or Italian like a native. To speak it like a native means doing things with your face, your lips, your hands, shoulders and whole body which are quite alien to the British nature. Scandinavians and Germans speaking perfect English are fine, because we require of them nothing remotely theatrical. Indeed I almost admire Britons who clearly have mastered the grammar and vocabulary of a language but continue to use them with both typical British *body* language and dignity of the facial muscles. Speak the language as if you had a nylon stocking over your head. Mr Heath, when prime minister, remained my hero when he went on TV to broadcast to the French nation, opening with the cut glass words 'Bonjour. *Je suis le prom-ee-aar dangler-taar . . .*' Great. The Queen makes a bit more effort, but happily stays well within acceptable British standards of restraint.

Extreme southern Mediterranean-style body language therefore is clearly out, which in some ways is a pity. It at least has the merit of being able to be easily understood, read and deployed – rather like a tick-tack man at the racetrack or trader on a commodity market. British body language is far subtler stuff, closer to a Sotheby's auction room than White City dog track or the trader's pit. The fact is, however, that to be a successful communicator you need to develop your body language skills as efficiently as you would expect to develop your written and spoken skills.

This need not be as difficult as it sounds. To succeed in most aspects of business life two facets of body language will be most called upon – attentive and submissive. Both generally appropriate to bosses and customers alike. In these situations a reflective response is best –

maintaining similar levels of eye contact, crossing and uncrossing legs, copying hand movements and adopting body positions in not too obvious synchronisation with them. All of this, along with being a good listener, and reflecting broadly similar views and tastes, generally succeeds.

You will have to develop your encoding and decoding skills. Encoding means being able to translate what you know the person wants from you into behaviour – rewards like sympathetic body posture, smiles, nods, grunts, appropriate eye contact and the rest, including the physical distance we stand or sit from them. For Britons a distance of, say, one and a half to three feet is fairly intimate, and should be reserved for close friends. Three to five feet seems about right to me for strangers and business contact. Try the cocktail party waltz some time. Stand a foot too close to some stranger you find yourself talking to and you will see that he or she will soon move back to re-establish what they feel is the right distance. Close the gap again yourself, and see how long it takes you to waltz them unknowingly once around the room.

Other nations – like the Latins – have different distance tolerances to the northern Europeans, and I think most Americans. In Japan, of course, two people keeping at least a body length away is not a question of manners but of survival – if they don't they will brain themselves each time they bow together.

Submissiveness is difficult for some people to swallow, as will be discussed later, but it is an important part of business and social life. We all use it, from pleading with traffic wardens not to give us tickets to the soccer stars hanging their heads to referees to avoid a booking. I used it once to dramatic effect in India where I was putting on an expensive audio-visual show to a big conference. Unfortunately, myself and my A/V crew had underestimated the truly Kafka-esque bureaucracy at Delhi airport and had been unable to get the equipment cleared through customs. We had gone past official closing time at the airport the night before the show, and the following day customs was closed for a national religious holiday. Our Indian agent had got us through every hoop but one, and now it seemed too late. Our van had even gone home, convinced we had no chance. Despite the late hour we went to this final point of clearance one last desperate time and, as our agent and the official ferociously argued in Hindi, I risked a bit of theatrics and muttered something about please help us, and performed the Indian gesture for 'please', hands held stiffly before the face in prayer form, and then the head and shoulders bowed. The customs official watched me and searched my eyes to see if I was being facetious or patronising, but when he saw I was in deadly earnest he suddenly grinned, stamped our form and somehow we got the equipment out. We transported it all the way to the five-star Taj Hotel on a cart pulled by two bullocks.

This was in 1984, just a few days before Mrs Gandhi was assassinated by Sikhs in her bodyguard, and the ensuing bloodbath. My show went on, thanks to my smart bit of body language, but I would not have wanted to have tried my hand at anything more serious. Political hostages or those abducted by psycopaths, sex offenders and other kidnappers certainly need all the help they can get from their accumulated experience of dealing with hostility and danger.

I once heard a police chief advise men who find themselves the subject of a random attack by a gang of high-spirited youths to sit on the floor and cry pathetically, offering no resistance nor challenge. There is a fair chance, he thought, that they might treat you as beneath contempt, not worth the loss of face involved in hitting such a whimp. A northern nightclub has a dwarf as a bouncer – 'There's no glory in hitting a midget,' says the manager.

(You really do hear conflicting advice on what to do when threatened. Prior to a business trip to Australia's Gold Coast, I decided I needed a contingency plan in the event of a shark attack when swimming. Consulting my normal source to give me a bluffer's knowledge of the jetset world – my collection of James Bond books – I learned that the trick with big predator fish is not to panic, as fear communicates itself through the water. You should establish instead a quiet orderly pattern of behaviour, not show confusion nor act chaotically. It seems that in the sea, ragged behaviour means the victim is out of control and vulnerable. Look like a bigger, more dangerous fish than the shark or barracuda eyeing you up. 'A thrashing fish is everyone's prey' it says in Ian Fleming's *Thunderball*, as 007 swims out to the Disco Volante.

Fine. It seems to make good sense. Until that is I talked to an Australian girl who told me she was swimming off the Great Barrier Reef one day with her brother, when they found themselves being circled by blue sharks. They did what *they* had been taught, which was to put their heads under the water and shout whilst thrashing and splashing around to frighten them off. And it worked.)

Avoiding eye contact with threatening individuals or groups is always good advice. I generally take a window seat in planes, convinced that any hijackers would find it easier to pick on someone in an aisle seat first. But if an abduction does take place, there will probably be a need to develop a submissiveness relationship with the person. Experts on this subject warn against the Stockholm factor, where the person abducted developed a close, supportive relationship with the abductor. It is a fact, however, that well-developed inter-personal skills can in extreme situations like a hostage crisis save your life. The top police negotiators in this field could probably become chairmen of companies or prime ministers if they channelled their skills in a different direction.

# Private Lives : Public Affairs

## Knowing Left from Right

The two halves of the human brain are known as the right and left hemispheres, and the interplay between them is now believed to contribute significantly to the way we behave. Our nervous system connects to the brain in a crossed-over fashion – the left hemisphere controlling the right side of our body, and vice versa. Biologists and behavioural scientists have over recent years developed the view that there are further more substantial differences to the two hemispheres.

If you are right-handed, the left hemisphere is thought to be where the learning process takes place, where information, facts and experiences are taken in and sorted in a logical way. The right hemisphere deals more with our senses and feelings – our non-verbal side which is so important in developing winning human and business relationships. In his book *The Separated Hemispheres*, Roger W. Sperry suggests that our educational system, as well as science in general, has tended to neglect this important non-verbal form of intellect.

There are a number of ways to activate more of our right hemisphere, tapping our non-verbal intellect: to make the effort to like what we are doing and the people we are with, to be inquisitive and a good listener, to be more physically demonstrative and emotionally involved, and to avoid only talking about work or the job in hand to those around us by using small talk positively.

## Home Goals

Our physical appearance, demeanour and dress sense tell others a great deal about ourselves. So does our home and choice of partner.

If you are experienced and confident of your social skills, and those of your partner, if you have a longish track record of enjoyable, civilised dinner parties at home where relative strangers have mixed well, then the reciprocal dinner and cocktail party circuit can be an excellent way of drawing bosses into your world. If not – beware.

The extent to which employers and people around you generally really want to know anything about your home life is to reassure themselves that it is stable, unexceptionable and so non-threatening to them. Tell them enough to create that impression, then keep home life, spouses, children and hobbies well out of your working environment.

If situations arise which make this impossible then some serious thinking is called for. If the boss invites you and your spouse round for dinner or Sunday brunch, if for reasons I cannot imagine, you feel the need to invite your boss round to dine with you, or to go to the theatre and supper as a foursome, what to do? Your husband, wife, girlfriend, boyfriend, kids or labrador dog will suddenly be brought into sharp focus as appendages to yourself on that corporate mantelpiece. How will they seem, how will you seem to his or her spouse? It's all far too big a risk to contemplate. My advice is to make excuses, avoid the meeting at all costs. If you are already doing well at work, you have everything to lose and probably little to gain.

Dinners are mercifully rare, but cocktail parties with spouses are more common. These are manageable for all but the most extrovert and/or obnoxious spouse, if they agree to sublimate themselves to you, speak when they are spoken to, are well briefed and drink little to nothing.

What do you do, however, if dinner really is thrust upon you, and you objectively realise you have a potential problem in your spouse? I have seen people agonising through evenings like this many times. The stereotypes are easy enough to recognise.

The man who 'married too young', with a sheepish wife and children from the first year, a woman denied the outside stimulus of continuing in work and meeting people other than housewives, children and shop-keepers. Her traditional conditioning as a woman has taught her to be passive, which she knows now is not the thing. On the other hand she has not had the environment in which to develop her new post-feminism skills, and if she attempts suddenly to be more assertive she is more likely to come over as simply loud and abrasive. The money has gone into dressing him well – that's more important – and she either makes her own things or thinks that she can still get away with that Laura Ashley. Her conversation is limited to children, the home and schools – OK if the other people have similar aged children, at state schools.

The woman with a husband in another sphere of work – perhaps a teacher, college lecturer, professional man – who is resentful and dismissive about the commercial world she's gone into and feels the need to assert himself as nobody's inferior. He will have heard all the office gossip from her and probably views her work colleagues as petty fools, especially the boss.

What to do? All the earlier advice about dress, appearance, and pre-planning safe conversation topics remains valid, as does the cliché about keeping off subjects like sex, politics and religion. Keeping off the drink remains important – one of you has to drive, why not make that the excuse for the spouse to refrain from drinking too much? Play safe. Be bland – anyone can be bland if they realise it is important enough. Don't make it a kind of unspoken target of yours to be entertaining, and so be asked round again. Forget the Bloomsbury set, the Pre-Raphaelite Brotherhood, the Café Royal wits – Shaw, Wilde and the rest. The evening is there to be reconnoitred and got through safely like a minefield − not to be enjoyed other than on a superficial basis. And remember, you don't really want your boss to relax too much with you, for him to get a little too drunk, a little too indiscreet about office matters, a little too leering over your wife's modest cleavage. There lies danger − of your becoming a threat to him in the cold light of day, an embarrassment to have around. Like the countless secretaries who have been the victims of a bit of 'hands-on' experience by bosses in the computer room after the Christmas party − however good they are, the bosses are just going to hope they go sooner rather than later.

Whatever happens, don't rashly feel the need to invite them back to dine with you a few weeks later. Bosses asking people round dread the thought of reciprocity, through some ghastly meal of avocado prawns, coq-au-vin (always made *avec poule* and *sans coq* − the great mistake) washed down with Mateus Rosé or some sickly sweet supermarket Liebfraumilch, consumed sitting on some cheap red and white striped mock Georgian dining chairs, probably covered in children's chewing gum. Either that or some soya bean vegetarian muck with homemade privet leaf wine, eaten in a stripped pine kitchen the size of his sauna, listening all night to Malcolm Arnold, Michael Tippett or some other such modern rubbish, while the conspicuously adopted dogs'-home stray rogers his leg. This overstates the case perhaps, but the threat is real enough.

Just as dangerous is the risk that your home may be at the other extreme − especially if you or your spouse has some family money. Heaven help you if your house is more desirable than his, your daughter's pony grazing in the paddock, the vegetables all from your own twelve acres, your second car the equal of his first, the Spode, the Gallés, the Augustus John drawings, the Quad amp and pre-amp with the Lynn deck ('*so* much better than compact disc, and *British*'), the 1961 first-growth claret and XO cognac (he never knew brandy could taste like that), the Romeo and Juliets with those special long Upmann Havana cigar matches . . .

If you have married across class, to a partner without money and from a lower social group, then unless they have become upwardly mobile do not expect your boss to understand. Partners who militantly retain their working-class roots despite middle-class joint bank accounts can be the kind of inverted snobs that can easily cost you your career prospects. In fact, mixed-class marriages themselves face more difficulties than most and are more likely to end in divorce. This is exacerbated in those cases where the wife has married someone from a lower social group. Violence, wife beating, is also more likely. A study in America, reported by Dr Michael Argyle and Monika Henderson in their book *The Anatomy of Relationships**, suggests that 45 per cent of husbands were

*William Heinemann, London, 1985

violent when the wife was better educated, compared with nine per cent when the husband was better educated or when they were equal.

## Knowing Others

In the submissive and attentive roles appropriate for acceptance by bosses, customers and others with power over us, there needs to be a subtle but discernible master/servant role – at least in early meetings, after which, if all goes well, something much closer to a peer group relationship can evolve. The master/servant role is based on the theory that people with power and authority welcome unprompted recognition of the distinction. It lightens the need for them to use difficult value judgements on how far they have to openly assert that authority.

Indeed there is evidence from some psychologists that successful relationships generally can best be built upon dominance from one party and submissiveness from the other. Dr Robert Winch, in his work *The Modern Family*, published in 1952, reflects the view that this can be the key to successful marriages and other close partnerships, with one person complementing the more forceful other person.

Of course the degree of submissiveness appropriate will vary dramatically from an urbane, broadminded boss or customer to the *'petit caporal'* variety, and your response may have to vary from Permanent Secretary to Junior Minister, from Cardinal to weak Pope, at one extreme, to as much Uriah Heep as you can stomach or carry off credibly. Clearly doing some homework on the people prior to important first meetings will pay dividends. Find out what you can about their age, educational background, marital status, any children, previous jobs, their origins (Northerner, Southerner, Scot, whatever), any hobbies or hobby horses, have they written on anything in the trade press in the last year, their politics even. Buy lunch for someone who works for them – most people enjoy a spot of whining and dining. It all helps, both in how to present yourself and in taking the 'reflective response' so useful with peer groups one step further – that is, to anticipate their responses, to put yourself firmly in their territory and have them reflecting back from you, demonstrating you are 'their kind of man' from the start.

Playing people correctly is perhaps the most important area – alongside appearance – where The Twenty Per Cent Factor can be gained. There are many examples. Using the right language, clearly taking the trouble to learn something of someone else's culture, is one. Whilst this is obviously true of foreign languages, it can equally be true of that common language which divides us from the USA. Jimmy Carter, on his first visit to the UK as the new American president, won many hearts and a lot of popularity when he called out to an audience of people in Newcastle, 'Away the lads!' – a local soccer chant.

Carlyle said that a great man shows his greatness by the way he treats little men. The first time I met Harold Wilson, when he was prime minister, he said, 'Hello, we've met before, haven't we?' I said that we hadn't and shook his hand. The next time I met him, a year later, he said, 'Hello, we've met before, haven't we?' It may have been a device to make the little men like me feel important, but it worked, and I respected him for taking the trouble.

You must also always try to put yourself in the shoes of the person you are trying to influence. Find out their needs, and see how best you can meet them by repackaging what you have to offer.

For example, the organisers of a pop music festival on the Isle of Wight in the early 1970s were very keen to attract the elusive Bob Dylan. Try as they may, nothing seemed to work. Then they discovered that Dylan was a great fan of the poet Tennyson, who had lived for a period on the island. This provided the bait which finally brought the star over.

You have to research people, however informally, and find out their interests and motivations. Generally speaking, they will only do things they want to do. To get them to do what *you* want them to do requires your finding plausible reasons for their self-interest, to marry together with your own. You must find common ground with the other person, something however small upon which you agree, then build on this carefully laid foundation of agreement. Once again, begin by demonstrating you are 'their kind of man' from the start.

There are many subtle ways to achieve this. For example, most bosses or customers can be divided into any variety of small but important categories such as being 'Mr' or Christian name people straight off, or being 'jackets off' people. Both of these small clues are easy enough to find out beforehand. Other clues are that some people are down to business straight away, followed perhaps by a few pleasantries and small talk; whilst others like to use small talk in the dog-sniffing way to open, for them subsequently to decide when to curtail things and get down to the job in hand.

Handshakes, in my experience, are a disappointing indicator of anything much, other than perhaps membership of the Brotherhood. Having a handshake myself like a limp if at least dry lettuce, I have experienced and endured bonecrushers and wet-fish jobs which have told me nothing at all about the people on the other end. The bonecrushers seem to like you muttering something about rugby prop forwards, but apart from that I can be of little further help in this area, which seems to me ripe for some original research by somebody.

Small talk is, however, very important. Never approach an important meeting without at least three or four carefully selected business and non-business topics which you can offer as runners to open, close, or fill any awkward silences. You really must be able to bat several easy balls into their court to relax them and make them feel at ease with you. Some of these topics will be selected from your intelligence gathering on the person or people beforehand, others from scanning the quality press for relevant snippets. You will know, of course, the trade topics high in their minds – raw materials prices, the exchange rate, whatever; a comment on the Test match score or British Rail's timekeeping if they are commuters might cover the non-business side.

If you are meeting in the person's office, a quick scan can give you clues to additional possible topics of relevance. Look for any photographs – of a spouse, children, car, the house perhaps as a backdrop, of a boat, the person playing some sport or other. Conversation hooks there perhaps on schools, school fees, gardening, sport, and so on. If they have framed certificates on the wall for professional qualifications or attendance at international conferences, there can be more clues here. Most people do not exhibit their certificates and those who do are probably active supporters of their institutes, and probably current or past office bearers, taking *industry* issues very seriously, not flippantly like some who flit from one sector to another.

Gadgets and executive toys might give you some indication of the person behind the job title, as may any pictures, non office-issue paintings and calendars. The tidiness of the desk can be a very good insight. Some companies' office house rules insist all desks be cleared at night as a matter of routine security, and so tidiness which seems universal there will tell you little. If on the other hand the desk seems perpetually tidy or untidy by the inclination of its owner, then his manner of working may prove to be methodical, highly professional to nit-picking in the case of the former; intuitive, all-in-the-head, creative to scatty in the case of the latter.

The person's secretary and/or personal assistant can also be clues themselves, as it is likely if the person has been in the job some time that he or she will have chosen them. Helpful, friendly, warm secretaries/PAs, with a sense of humour or fun, are likely to reflect their bosses. Beware of tycoons/aspirant tycoons, however, who have servile PAs, probably with MBAs, who get in the way of you getting close to the boss. Normally bright young men, they seem to spend most of their time giving the tycoon's latest estimated time of arrival from talking to the chauffeur on the car phone. They recall to me the practice of plain Roman princesses who used to carry an ugly monkey around with them to make themselves seem more beautiful by comparison. When with their boss, the worst type of PA seems to echo his or her sentiments and act as a human transmitter and amplifier of their boss's moods, being able to read them much more quickly than anyone else – clucking and frowning far more disapproval than the tycoon could afford to show with dignity, and being far more gay about the unfreezing of a little sardonic corporate humour.

It's a difficult and thankless role. I was policy co-ordinator to the President of the Confederation of British Industry for a number of years, working with a great many senior industrialists. I hope and believe I never fell into the trap of becoming a kind of thinking man's batman of the type I have described, but as an ex-insider I do think that PAs say more about their boss than about themselves. Certainly secretaries and PAs are useful guides to the boss's temperament, and can be powerful friends or enemies later. Make sure you get on with them and make sure your own secretary does too. Don't let a pompous or rude secretary of your own give others the impression she is reflecting *your* personality.

Given the security mania of most companies today, another clue to spotting as many straws in the wind as possible is to cast an eye when you sign in at reception at who else has been visiting your target earlier that day. It may have been one of your competitors or another supplier whose work and products you know. Useful intelligence.

Accents are another clue. A studiously retained regional dialect in someone long outside their home area is generally a sign that BBC Radio 3 accents and Chelsea phraseology will not go down well. Equally a genuine or acquired Eton-Ox-Guards approach will call for some pretty swift reflective responsing by those of us from *oop* North.

Dialect – Scottish, Welsh, Cornish, Yorkshire or from wherever – may give a lead to some small talk or gentle banter. Mannerisms in speech may trigger off in you some feeling of precognition. It always seems to me that people who cannot, or rather will not, pronounce the letter 'r' as anything other than a 'w' are of a type – self-perceived social or intellectual patricians. I'm convinced it is simply an affectation, inherited or otherwise. Wonald Weagan wunning for Pwesident all those years ago has made them even more conspicuous than usual.

Class first raises its head very often with accents. Those of us with deep insecurities about class find themselves in a minefield when confronted with real or imagined potential snobbery. It is the one field of first impressions/human relations where I still feel very exposed and inadequate. An immature phase many go through – including me – is that of becoming an inverted snob, of feigning scorn for anyone other than down-to-earth self-made people. But it really doesn't wash. It can be a schoolchild, a graduate, an estate agent, or a businessman in his sixties. Age or career status has little to do with the ability of some people with social breeding to reduce the likes of me to feeling like an upstart barely out of the primaeval soup, or an aspirant parvenu on a good day.

There are any number of subtle ways they can do this – from probings about schools, home, father's occupation, from name dropping, from the use of coded language (it's racing, never *horse* racing) and assorted bits of Latin and Greek. I may have graduated from mushy peas to mushy mange-tout, but nothing short of a cultural lobotomy is ever going to help me out of this particular swirling sea of personal insecurities. However, fill the role they have decided for you. If the prize is big enough and worth it, I find my only way of getting through is to know my place. If the rich could hire the poor to die for them, the poor would make a good living . . .

In turn, people with a cultured accent and breeding can find themselves equally exposed when looking for jobs outside the usual hunting grounds of the City, the forces, estate management, the law and other professions. I know they can feel just as vulnerable to being unfairly pigeon-holed as effete, stuck-up and chinless by inverted snobs, when they themselves are looking for employment or orders from customers. Britain remains far from a meritocracy, and the nastier respective sides of the class divide have to be acknowledged. Time and familiarity can overcome them, but those important first impressions will have to be tackled. Know yourself.

Empathy in these many and varied forms is practised naturally by anyone good at inter-personal skills. It may not be a pure science, but it is at least subject to the mathematics of probabilities. Naturally maturity and experience help enormously, but it should be remembered that the mind is more sophisticated and faster than any computer, and most people you meet actually want the meeting to go well, so much is on your side.

Being successful in human relations terms, however, is hard work, and not nearly so haphazard or unscientific as most people believe. It really is not good enough any longer to put failures down to having to deal with impossible people, irrational people, morons, snobs or bigots. *You* are the real problem through your own laziness, unpreparedness and lack of application.

## Modern Social Influences

There are a variety of influences which you may detect in the people with whom you are having to deal which have arisen from relatively recent social changes. The rapid progress towards sexual and racial equality is one. Divorce is another.

First, equality. Most middle-aged and older women will have been brought up by parents with traditional views on the role of women, in a society which set, shaped and shared those views. As we know, things have changed – particularly in larger cities and in the higher socio-economic groups. But even if sexism had totally disappeared – which of course it has not – women of this age have still had to undergo a transition from their passive role-models, which for many will have been traumatic. This is especially true of working mothers, single-parent or otherwise, but perhaps especially working mothers by choice, where despite themselves a pervading sense of guilt at turning their back on 'a woman's place' continues to gnaw at them. All of this may make them sensitive, brittle and humourless on predictable topics, but very receptive to genuine recognition of what they see as some of their burdens. A woman director I know, after many years on the board, still says eyes turn to her when a tea tray is brought in or a telephone needs answering.

Minorities – racial, sexual, people with disabilities – have faced over the same period similar shifts in social attitudes. Anti-semitism remains the great Christian disease, and colour prejudice will also make us all the poorer for decades to come. I remember some years ago, whilst working for the Textile Council in Manchester, becoming concerned at the implications of the very high percentages of Asian people working in spinning mills on some aspects of factory management. A majority did not have English as a first language and it occurred to me that, as an industry, it would be prudent to recognise this by, for example, having fire and machine safety signs written in Urdu, Hindi, Gujarati or whatever, and possibly training manuals and even contracts of employment. I spent a morning in vain on the telephone trying to find mill owners who had already done something along these lines, when finally one man laughed down the line at me and said proudly that yes, he did have a sign in Urdu – it said 'No vacancies'.

## National Stereo-typecasting

Every generation, including our own, seems to feel the need to stereotype races and nationalities. We joke in Britain about the Irish, the Americans about the Poles, and so on. The British also have knee-jerk reactions to the French, the Japanese, Australians, Germans and Arabs. Most of us know it is wrong and probably believe that deep down we are not really influenced by it.

I am far from sure it is anything like as innocent as all that. National and racial stereo-typecasting is a strong force – on ourselves and on those foreign nationals we meet who know how, say, the Brits perceive them. It is difficult for any generation to judge itself in this respect, and so I delved into recent history to see how our great-grandfathers viewed the world. See how shocking the following entries now seem to us. They are taken from *Beeton's Dictionary of Universal Information*, an early kind of household encyclopedia published about a hundred years ago. Remember, they would have been written by highly educated experts on their subject – not the common man in the street.

**Russians.** 'The manners of the people are, in general, far from cleanly. Drinking is a very common vice among them. Gambling is also prevalent. The Russian peasantry are in a very abject condition; and, morally speaking, the nobles are ignorant, proud, sensual and generally devoid of principle. The lower orders are equally coarse in their appetites, and, in many situations, equally open to charges of deceit and falsehood.'

**Irish.** 'That part of the inhabitants called the Wild Irish were formerly as savage as the native Americans and, like them, lived in huts, making a fire in the middle of them; but it is to be hoped that all the rude and barbarous customs, as well as every other trace of wretchedness and degradation, will vanish in time, and that a general industry will take the place of beggary . . .'

**Chinese.** 'Their greatest and best good quality is a steady and unremitting industry. To balance this, however, they exhibit all the vices of mean and degraded minds. From the throne to the lowest subject, an utter and abhorrent disregard of truth prevails, and their unrivalled skill in every branch of the art of cheating, has been remarked, with astonishment, by all their mercantile visitors.'

**Egyptians.** 'The complexion of the Egyptians is tawny, and as we proceed southward they become darker, until those near Nubia are almost black. They are generally indolent and cowardly. The richer sort do nothing all day but drink coffee, smoke tobacco, and sleep, and they are ignorant, proud, haughty and ridiculously vain.'

**Persians** (Iranians). They get a better press – 'gay, lively and active. There is no country where the beard is regarded with such veneration, it being repeatedly during the day washed, combed and adjusted. They are the most learned people in the East . . .' But even here there is a sting in the tail – 'morality is much studied in Persia, though little practised.'

**Portuguese.** You may have thought that our oldest ally would have fared well. Not so. 'The women in the capital are loose and dissolute; in the country the people are indolent and listless. A want of cleanliness is equally complained of in the capital and in the provincial towns.'

Have we changed much? Do we not still stereotype people in this way, and are we not still influenced by a century of patrician brainwashing, the masses accepting the prejudices of the very few who had ever travelled?

There are prejudices nearer to home. Some Scottish people are pointedly racist towards the English. Some Welsh extremists commit arson on English people's homes in their country. I was born in Salford and immediately found myself stereotyped in three important tribal ways – I was Protestant (or more accurately I was not Roman Catholic); the people around me supported Manchester United not Manchester City; and people like us voted Labour ('only people with shops and the rentman vote Tory').

I can also recall later in life a friend of mine, who had been transferred from a factory in Lancashire to another in the group in Yorkshire, refusing to let his heavily pregnant wife move to Yorkshire until the baby was born a Lancastrian.

You are going to have to identify and cope with these kinds of innocent and serious prejudices not just in others important to you, but in yourself.

If you have some degrees of prejudice within you of a racial kind or against, say, homosexuals, then you will already find yourself being forced to come to terms with it because of social pressures, and the influence of the media and legislation. Even then, however, in new encounters you must understand the suspicions minorities will have from the kicks they will have endured throughout their lives. You will have to avoid unintentional insults which arise through your own conditioning – like opening up conversations with Asian people by asking about cricket, or about boxing with black people.

Happily most bigots are cowardly and only express their intolerances against groups of people, not against individuals who have that annoying habit of not fitting their stereotype, of having feelings just like themselves and frequently actually being rather nice.

Almost as bad as bigotry, however, is any hint of patronisation – intended or not. Behave normally. In due course, when you have got to know people, you *should* ask or comment on, say, the problems of their getting around in a wheelchair, on their heritage or religion, unless they have somehow warned you off the subject. That is behaving normally too.

Minorities, people who society may have on occasions treated unkindly, will generally be a more cynical audience for you. So will our next group – the growing army of divorced people.

## The Divorcynics

About a quarter of all marriages in the UK now end in divorce, and about a third of recent marriages break up. Over half of divorces involve dependent children, and over half remarry. By the end of the century, a quarter of the people in the UK will have been affected by a broken marriage or a divorce. In 1970 the number of divorces in relation to marriages was fourteen per cent, in 1980 it was forty per cent, in 1985 forty-six per cent.

The average marriage in England lasts just nine years. More than a third of new marriages break up, although a third of those divorced remarry within two and a half years.

Divorce, along with bereavement and moving house, is one of the three most stressful times in life – although a friend of mine maintains that a Pickfords' van running over his 'ex' would cheer him up no end. The disappointment and bitterness of a broken marriage tend to make the sufferers less trusting and more cynical – after all, if the person they chose to live the rest of their lives with has let them down, what might *you* or your company do to them? The word 'divorcynic' was first coined by researchers working on a project commissioned by Wasey-Campbell-Ewald from the Social Futures Group of the Henley Centre and research consultants Holder and Scorah. This research showed how divorcees were more sceptical than most about advertising and marketing – people selling to them.

You will not change people who feel this way, but you may have a better chance of packaging yourself and your wares to them more attractively if you are aware of this possible dimension to their personality.

# The Business of Morality

## Philosophy

If, like me, you had always thought philosophy to be about as interesting as a drum solo, then the analysis so far of how we make and form impressions should call for a rethink. The word philosophy derives from the Greek for the love of wisdom, and wisdom is the core of all successful decisions and judgements.

The problem with philosophy is that on a superficial level it can sound so crass. Take Descartes' famous assertion, *Cogito, ergo sum* – 'I think, therefore I am.' Or Aristotle's definition of truth – 'To say of what is that it is not, or what is not that it is, is false, while to say of what is that it is, or is not that it is not, is true.' Got it? Both of these famous statements are cornerstones of epistemological discussion, but do they and does classical philosophy have a relevance to modern business and social life?

It will be clear by now that the seemingly innocuous business of public relations, of becoming an efficient transmitter and receiver of overt and covert messages, is in fact extremely complex. An understanding of some of the philosophical debates which go to the heart of human understanding can not only help us 'know ourselves' better, but also help us to know how opinions are formed in the first place.

Western philosophy has three broad movements: epistemology, ethics and metaphysics. With an arbitrariness that would make Sartre turn in his existentialist grave, I will dismiss metaphysics (as he did) as the least obviously relevant for business and general social purposes. That still leaves the many strands of epistemology and ethics, however, which have filled minds and bookshelves for centuries past. Distilling a manageable handful of key messages from the legacy calls for even greater arbitrariness. At least the nihilists will applaud me.

Epistemology is the study of our grounds for knowledge and beliefs. It looks, in an intellectually disciplined manner, at the concepts of knowledge and wisdom. What is the relationship between knowledge, truth and belief? Can knowledge exist independently of a 'knower'?

Ethics studies the science of morality and looks at why and how decisions are made – for pleasure (hedonism), for the greatest good for the greatest number (utilitarianism), for peace of mind (epicureanism), for the will of god (religion), because it will have the desired practical consequences (pragmatism), as a result of previous experience (empiricism), because we know what to do from some kind of internal pre-programming within us (rationalism) . . .

And you thought you just drank a glass of water because you were thirsty. Philosophy and philosophers, of course, are easy targets for ridicule – Voltaire at least did it with style. But it is a great mistake to let the jargon and apparent irrelevance blind you to their practical use in life.

For me there are two main strands running through philosophies with which we come in day to day contact.

The first is empiricism, founded largely on the work of two British philosophers. John Locke, in his *Essay Concerning Human Understanding*, published in 1690, argued that our mind is a blank tablet (*tabula rasa*) and that all our ideas come from impressions taken from our senses. David Hume, in his *A Treatise of Human Nature*, published almost fifty years later, developed empiricism still further, drawing the distinction between impressions and ideas. He believed that impressions (are the pennies starting to drop yet?) have more influence on us than ideas.

The second main strand comes a few years later in the eighteenth century from Immanuel Kant, who we will meet again later. He argued instead the existence in all of us of 'a priori' knowledge, not linked to learning or observation by the senses or by experience. You cannot discuss ethics without considering the conscience.

The dominant and essentially unsound philosophy of modern business and political life remains utilitarianism, developed by Jeremy Bentham from his *Principles of Morals and Legislation*, published in 1789. The greatest happiness for the greatest number philosophy is still the way on which most governments, legal codes, big firms and indeed family units are run. It certainly has its critics. Kant for one, with his 'categorical imperative' belief that absolute right should never be modified for the sake of expediency. Today's conviction politician for another, and some bosses and military leaders who have their own clear views on what constitutes the 'right' course of action, and will pursue it regardless of consequences. Certainly utilitarianism untouched by intuition has no answer for morality.

My own back-of-envelope eclectic philosophy is to write the word 'conscience', Kant's moral imperative, on Locke's blank tablets. Kant's position on moral issues alongside Locke's empiricism gives me a way to intellectualise what I do and why. What life has taught me, however, is that some other people, and some organisations, have different values to my own and hence requirements and ways of operating. You need to understand and recognise this. In some, their conscience seems to play a remarkably insignificant role (as in many criminals – Cesare Lombroso was not all wrong); in others, their conscience is more selective, depending on whether they are operating in developed or Third World nations. Things have improved, but the philosophical stance in the past of some multi-nationals can only be likened to that of old-style colonial powers. Acceptance of inalienable rights seemed to vary to the square of the distance between the urbane head office and the outpost. The row in

West Germany early in 1987 over plans to export to Third World countries 3,000 tons of milk powder said to be radioactive as a result of the
Chernobyl nuclear accident, shows the issue in high relief still. The West
German health minister is reported as saying it was 'unethical,
irresponsible and morally reprehensible' to discriminate between the
health of Europeans and the peoples of developing countries. The
philosophical stance of certain business sectors can be very different
from others – the arms industry, tobacco industry and some sides of the
pharmaceuticals business (the legal and illegal drugs industries) are
three of the most extreme examples which can have more to do with
pragmatism than epicureanism.

Those of us with an active conscience go through life being regularly
surprised and disappointed by the actions of others not so blessed or
damned. On a small scale we are all aware of petty thieving in any
working environment – from fiddling expenses to making free with
company postage stamps, stationery or telephones, and this from people
who would no more steal a box of matches from a corner shop than they
would hold up a bank. They are the kind of people, however, who
*always* 'lose' a cheap camera on holiday every year, to the approximate
value of their holiday insurance premium.

When working in the holiday industry I once took a call from a man
who asked me how far 'far' was. I asked him to explain and he said that
he had a holiday brochure which said a certain hotel was not far from the
beach. How far is 'not far'? Without seeing the brochure in context I said
I didn't know, to which he replied that he did; 'not far' in fact was almost
two kilometres. He knew because he had found another brochure from
another company which featured the same hotel, saying it was that
distance from the beach. The man proudly told me that he intended to
book with the operator who said it was 'not far' and, as he suffered from
angina, would demand free taxis to and from the beach every day when
he got there, plus compensation on his return.

On a grander scale, the need to win can be used to justify so many
dubious attitudes and actions. The irony is that the competitive culture
which seems to be a prerequisite for democratic government and for
consumer prosperity, calls for that dangerous brew of ambition, aggression and single-mindedness in its heroes and heroines. And is there
anything more elitist than unbridled meritocracy? And is not relatively
unbridled competition between international companies simply a kind
of multi-national battle of the meritocratic giants playing for world
stakes? This is a form of war, and if truth is its first casualty then you can
be sure it won't be the last. If the war parallel is accepted – as it is by
most of the combatants – then ordinary, social standards of behaviour
and morality will be set aside.

The contrast is most easily seen reflected in the mellowing of tycoons
once they have made their pile. With more than half an eye on some
quango, knighthood or peerage (nothing less), they throw themselves

and their shareholders' money into charities and political activities. Still feeling tainted as robber barons, they embark on the pursuit of 'respectability' and a 'Lady' prefix for their latest wife (typically the second or third by now) with all the zeal they used to reserve for the market place.

The truth is, however, that it is not they who are out of step within Western society, but society with them. This peculiar breed of tunnel-visioned, workaholics create – through self-interest – wealth and jobs for us all as well as fortunes, enemies, broken marriages and heart conditions for themselves. The British honours system would be a more honest reflection of the *realpolitik* of British life if it honoured these people earlier and for their *real* work rather than giving it to them later in life for phoney reasons. At present, some twenty per cent of honours go to public sector time-servers whose only understanding of wealth creation is their inflation-proof pension. Britain was more honest in respect of adventurers, for that is what true entrepreneurs are, in Elizabethan times, in the days of Drake and Raleigh. Raleigh – has there ever since been such a man of culture and adventure: could he exist today? He perhaps could only truly prosper during the first Elizabeth's reign; after her he spent most of his life in the Tower and, following a failed search for gold along the Orinoco, he was executed by that post-Elizabethan version of the offenders' short, sharp shock treatment – the axe.

Now, rather than gathering around in crowds at public executions of heroes and villains, the weak, the mediocre and the envious gather around their TV screens and read their magazines and newspapers with glee as tycoons occasionally get their come-uppance on tax, fraud, insider dealing, sex, drinks or drugs charges – and it remains an equally unedifying facet of human nature.

If patriotism (or morality or any of the other versions) is the last refuge of the coward, the moral indignation of the masses at today's adventurers is surely the last refuge of the faint-hearted who still, nonetheless, buy their products or derive their livelihood from them.

I said my own eclectic philosophy was a mixture of Kant's a priori conscience and Locke's empiricism. To put it less pretentiously – whatever lets you sleep at night. This is not as flip as it sounds. You must know yourself and how far you are prepared to stray from your own vision of acceptable business and social behaviour. For most of us this is a one-lane country B-road, not the American-style five-lane freeways of the real adventurers. The concise Oxford Dictionary defines a freeway as an express highway with limited access. Limited access for the few; dangerous and difficult to get off. But don't despise the brave – without them we would have to accept a materially lower standard of living. Don't copy them either. You will not be able to loosen the reins on your conscience and live with yourself as comfortably. This is one area where the Twenty Per Cent Factor does not work. You are stuck with your own moral imperative – live within it contentedly, but do not make the mistake of so many puritans and see it as an imperative to moralise at others.

## Integrity

Our work, social and family duties take up most of our waking hours, and they are all too important for us to fake it for long with any of them. You cannot pretend you like, let alone love, somebody for any length of time without them realising it, you cannot treat family responsibilities simply as a kind of duty without others – old people and children especially – noticing your hearty but phoney front. Animals spot it too. I don't like dogs much, and most of them snap at me if I attempt a friendly pat to please their owners.

Just so with your working environment. Your customers, workmates and bosses soon realise who is *really* interested in working with them, and who is just going through the motions. And it matters. It matters most of all with customers, and in selling, because customers can literally take us or leave us. Of course, salesmen and women want our business and are generally just trying to sell us one service or product. Yet I have met life assurance, encyclopedia and double-glazing salespeople who I knew had a real belief in their product and enjoyed their work. We have all met the other kind, too, the people who make us feel like their audience in the sales training school and who display all manner of subliminal signals which tell us they don't believe what they are saying – the wrong amount of eye contact (far too much or far too little), the invasion of our space, the use of sales props and manufactured deadlines of impending tax changes or price rises to force-feed us with their pap.

One technique used by some financial services salespeople is to lure you off your home territory and into their offices, literally to have you sit in a corner, where they bring their own chair too close to you, making you want to do something to escape (like signing something, anything). They talk *at* you, and when they come to the punch line (say, about what happens to your wife if you die . . .) they need direct eye contact for maximum impact and memorability, so they use a prop (a pen, or better still their spectacles) to lift your eyes directly into their own, and then bang – out comes the pithy message, the tiny percentage of all they have said which they know you will then remember.

There is nothing wrong with the act of selling – that is what much of this book is about – nor is there anything wrong in analysing what approach will work best to meet your objective (that is what all of this book is about). But technique must not be obvious or, no matter how strong the message, the delivery mechanism may turn our audience off. The same is true in the arts – if an actor's, pianist's or dancer's technique gets in the way of the piece they are performing, then it is the technique which we are most aware of, not the piece itself.

At least a conspicuous technique is a sign that someone cares enough to have trained thoroughly. The worst of all is the lack of integrity that goes with an 'I don't care' attitude. It is best illustrated in the behaviour of some shop assistants, builders and plumbers, and in the nationalised industries and public utilities which have near monopolies. No less common, however, is this same attitude in some people in virtually any organisation you can name – malcontents, people who feel passed over, jealous of others or who are genuinely in the wrong job or career.

Uncommitted, badly-managed young shop assistants working for companies associated with failure can hardly be blamed. By changing the corporate culture, and by retraining, they can be helped. As for the rest, the only solution is to fire them or encourage them to leave and find fulfilment and happiness elsewhere. It would not be a cheap sop to say you are really helping them by firing them – you probably are. As for yourself, don't invest your energies in trying to turn around or hang on to no-hopers. You will almost always fail, and make yourself depressed in the process. Let them go, but concentrate on the average to good people. You can make them twenty per cent happier, more committed and more productive over a short space of time. What's more you would enjoy it and get tremendous personal fulfilment from it too. Never underestimate that side of the equation. Mission impossibles will only drive you into a depression and cost you your confidence – a delicate flower for most of us.

And there is a word missing in most discussions about business life. Fun. What's more, if the right breeding ground can be made, it is highly infectious.

The chairman of a big holiday company tells the story of how he makes a habit of sitting in his reservations department most Saturday mornings with his finance director, taking bookings. One day he made a slip of some kind and the travel agent rang back to clarify things. On this occasion he got through to the finance director who, to the delight of all the reservation clerks around, apologised, saying that the lad who took the first call only worked there on Saturdays.

In the same company the spirit in the complaints department – a tough and stressful job – is kept high by this kind of fun, but hard-working, corporate attitude. The head of the unit was away for a couple of weeks and her in-tray had been steadily growing, a miserable sight for anyone returning from holiday. One of the clerks noticed this, put a single Polo mint on the table and said, 'Right. Whoever clears the biggest number of her files gets the mint.' Good-naturedly everyone joined in and cleared the backlog, with no need for big sticks or big incentives.

Integrity and the enjoyment of life call for mutual respect and, I believe, shared values and goals. Transcendentalist Ralph Waldo Emerson, in his book *Representative Men*, captured the spirit of this beautifully in a mood of optimistic humanism:

*If there is love between us, inconceivably delicious and profitable will our intercourse be; if not, your time is lost, and you will only annoy me. I shall seem to you stupid, and the reputation I have false. All my good is magnetic, and I educate not by lessons, but by going about my business.*

## Wolves at the Door

Another way to try and achieve a more united spirit is to create or over-emphasise the threat of a common enemy – the domestic competition, the Japanese entering the market 'to do to us what they did to our motorcycle industry', an unwanted takeover, the threat of national-isation, the threat of some new British or EEC law or tax, and so on.

The wolf at the door is an old tactic and not one to be lightly dismissed.

The Soviet Union is no real union at all. There is strong but surpressed opposition to the dominance of Moscow in many of the fifteen republics and regions across the vast continent and, in places like Georgia and Kazahkstan, nationalistic feelings just as strong as those of some of the Irish, Scots, Basques, Palestinians, Corsicans, and Sikhs elsewhere in the world – as well as dissension from human-rights activists, Jews and others. As for the Soviet satellites, the events over the past thirty years in countries like Hungary (1956), Czechoslovakia (1968) and Poland (1981), not to mention Berlin, speak for themselves. One of the ways the unity is maintained is by keeping the memory of the last world war and its terrible human cost very much alive. Other siege mentality countries like Israel and South Africa do much the same. None of them is crying wolf. The beast *is* at the door. Let none of us ever forget the 18 million people lost by the Soviet Union in World War II alone. The question in the context of a book looking at management style is, does it work – does it lead to unity and everyone pulling productively together? My view is that it does not. The Soviet Union is notoriously inefficient in both its industrial and agricultural sectors. As for countries where to varying degrees opposition parties are allowed, the wolves without Israel and within and without South Africa have not created political or social unity. Fear is an imperfect master: everyone wants to escape and cheat him.

## The Dunkirk Spirit?

The much-vaunted Dunkirk spirit of war-torn Britain is often quoted as an example of unity out of adversity. The classic pull together, there's a wolf at the door approach to management. Evidence suggests, however, that the threat imposed by Hitler failed to generate the degree of common spirit which is now held as accepted wisdom. At the start of the war, for example, the government asked the Trades Union Congress for assurances of support for the war effort. The TUC, in old negotiating style, put on the table amendments they wanted to the Trade Disputes Act, which concerns trade union recognition and privileges.

Following the coalition in May 1940, the Labour Party's Ernest Bevin became Minister of Labour and a panoply of legislation was put in place – the Emergency Powers (Defence) Act and Defence Regulation 58A, a supplement to existing negotiating machinery with the National Arbitration Tribunal and an Order in Council (Order 1305) which made strikes and employer's lock-outs unlawful. At the same time Bevin, following precedent from the First World War, gave statutory backing to guarantees that practices abandoned by unions during the emergency could be restored at the end of the war. This was done through the Restoration of Pre-War Practices Act, 1942.

As the phoney war ended and Britain became locked into real action, things at first looked good on the 'united we stand' front. The number of days lost by strikes fell in 1940 to the lowest on record. Even the British communists were rooting for industrial harmony and higher productivity to help beat the German threat to international socialism.

It didn't last long. Days lost through strikes in the years 1941–45 were higher than in 1938. Nineteen forty-four was the worst, recording more days lost than in any year since 1932. Strikes were about the usual peacetime things, mainly wages. In some key sectors there was a reluctance to work overtime, and wild-cat strikes were far from uncommon.

Take two of the industries most vital to the war effort – coal and shipbuilding.

The coal industry was responsible for half the days lost in 1943 and two-thirds those lost in 1944. One point two million man days and two million tons of coal were lost in the first quarter of 1944 alone. Bevin himself spoke out, saying that action by miners in the Sheffield area had inflicted more damage to the country's industry than a heavy air raid.

In shipbuilding there were severe problems arising from craft disputes between unions. In 1941, for example, there was a strike on the Clyde in the summer because of a dispute between the Boilermakers' Society and the Constructional Engineering Union, and another in 1944 on Tyneside when the Boilermakers insisted only their members could operate a new American flame-planing machine. All this despite the existence of the Restoration of Pre-War Practices Act. In the latter incident the strike continued even after the employers had withdrawn the machine from use, and the men had to be summoned and fined before they would return to work.

In a talk to the Royal Society of Arts in April, 1986, Correlli Barnett, author of *The Audit of War**, quoted figures for the aircraft industry, which had suffered from managerial problems as well as wild-cat strikes. Britain's peak annual productivity in structure weight per

*Macmillan, London, 1986

employee was four-fifths that of Germany and less than half that of America.

By spring 1944 wage rates generally had risen by around eleven per cent more than the cost of living – average earnings by more still due to overtime. By the end of the war total trade union membership had also risen substantially – from just over six million in 1938 (including 4.6 million affiliated to the TUC) to 7.8 million in 1945 (including 6.6 million affiliated).

Wartime parallels are quoted too often and too glibly. They have little relevance to modern life. The 'Dunkirk Spirit' has as much myth about it as the management styles of a Montgomery or Patton, and each has little to teach us when divorced from the emergency conditions in which they existed.

## Morality

Confidence tricksters and skilled gigolos can teach us a great deal about the advance preparation, intelligence gathering, rehearsal and invest-ment in charm that they deploy. I heard one old gigolo describe how he always put his hand on the woman's left breast as a first move to seduction, because that is the one normally used first to suckle children. Apparently this makes women feel less threatened. How many experi-mental hands up assorted jumpers led to that little gem, I will never know, but he seemed earnest and happy enough with his batting average.

The degree to which any individual wishes to use the deliberate manipulation of his or her appearance and personality in the ways I have described is a matter for personal judgements. Some people claim not to have the temperament to bend very far, although I suspect this is often used as a post-rationalised excuse to themselves and others for their failure. Others think it is just plain wrong to manipulate social relationships or their inter-personal skills in this way. Although that is the point really. You are not manipulating others, only yourself. People can and will form their own independent judgement of you or whatever it is you might be selling.

The people skilled at it are never seen to be bending at all of course, otherwise all is lost in any case.

Moral issues do arise however. Whilst empathising in pursuit of business success to Olympic gold medal standard, I have occasionally had to listen to racist, sexual and political remarks being made by people with opinions somewhere to the right of a Birmingham taxi driver. I'm right of centre on some issues myself, but these were views which would have got short shrift from me, for example, at a social gathering. My reaction? I would absorb them without comment and without any non-verbal cues that might show I disagreed. Perhaps you would have acted differently, but I maintain generally that would be wrong. *You* are representing your organisation, not yourself: *they* would have been reflecting their personal prejudices, not their organisation's. Let lying dogs sleep.

If on the other hand the nature of the company or product with which you are planning to deal is offensive to you, then you have the option to decline to get involved and take the consequences. I will not involve myself in promoting cigarettes, for example. In the very early days of a new public relations company which I helped found, we were invited to pitch jointly with another firm for the International Gold Corporation, a South African company which marketed krugerrands. We were not successful, but are ashamed of ourselves to this day for pitching in the first place. You can sell-in by selling out, but it has a price.

Much of this book is about succeeding, however, about people and organisations committed to meeting moderately ambitious goals. To achieve this means finding out and gauging what people important to you and your company want from you, and then giving them what they want. A price for that on occasions is to become a kird of corporate cushion, and go through life bearing the impression of the last person who sat on you.

Contrary to popular belief, winners are not leaders, they are the faithful servants of whatever market they are in. The market dictates and winners follow. The most successful people I know – tycoons and others – have a dignified servility to people and groups important to them that would shock most of the people who work for them.

# Common Barriers to Communication

If you have begun to know yourself, the next step is to know the kind of organisation in which you are operating and in which you would like to prosper. When you have assessed this you can see how best to package yourself to meet the real corporate goals, and to help the organisation achieve them.

For many organisations the biggest single obstacle for greater success is not the competition, nor poor trading conditions – it is themselves. The enemy within can come in many forms – company politics, low, defeatist morale, ham-fisted management, poor labour relations, acute demarcation problems, poor quality or half-hearted, uncommitted selling.

A survey carried out in 1986 by Korn/Ferry and *Scottish Business Insider* magazine into Scottish firms showed that sixty-two per cent felt their company's external image was the issue most likely to increase in importance that year. Financial results were the chief concern of fifty-four per cent of responses, followed by employee relations, cash flow, stockbroker relations, management succession and day to day operations. The typical company surveyed had sales of around £75 million a year, and more than a thousand employees. That Scottish companies – not trendy London and south-eastern firms – should rate aspects of public relations so highly in their immediate priorities is significant. It shows their boards know that something needs doing, that prudent financial control, budgeting, production efficiency and sales targets are not enough; that however well they think they are doing at the sharp end of their business, some mysterious ingredient 'x' is needed to bring it all together, perhaps to oil the rusty wheels of the success bandwagon and set it rolling again.

What they really need, of course, is to 'know themselves'. The solutions which follow from this are obvious enough.

## Sack the Managing Director

Conspicuously successful chief executives are quick enough to accept the credit for booming profits or for turnaround situations. It might be more helpful, however, if society instead pilloried and shamed their predecessors and people still in office like them. That we can each perhaps roll off only half a dozen names of top management heroes over the last 10–20 years only serves to underline the depressing fact that there have been so many second-raters running organisations which deserve better.

I think that one reason for the poor quality of so much of the now older generation of top management in industry and the public sector is the legacy of the two world wars. So many of the nation's potential leaders were lost during their war service, or returned to university or civilian business life after six difficult years to find that the 'essential workers', their erstwhile peer groups who stayed behind for any number of reasons, were three-quarters the way up the greased pole with knowledge and experience which made them virtually invincible. It would be interesting to know how many of the captains of industry and the civil service sporting knighthoods since the mid-1960s saw military service.

It has been estimated that the First World War claimed eight million lives in total, people who died in battle or from wounds or illness, with twenty-one million people injured. To put these ghastly astronomic figures into some sort of scale our minds can take, in one day (1 July 1916) in the Somme area Britain lost 19,240 men, half a generation of the country's male youth. This was the heaviest single day's casualties ever sustained by the British Army. The Battle of the Somme over four months cost 420,000 British lives.

The personal tragedies of course come first to mind. But what of the cost to a small island nation like Britain? In total the two world wars, over the space of thirty-one years, claimed over a million British lives and many more injured, the vast majority of them young males just approaching the prime of life. The very fabric of Britain, the supply of brain and brawn, the warp and weft of this fabric, was damaged perhaps irretrievably. Britain's role in the world would never be the same again; the heritage of the glorious Elizabethan age, the great Victorian industrial era, lost. As members of virtually the only British generation in history not to face conscription, or world or localised wars (Boer, Malaya, Kenya, Cyprus), people of my generation enjoying a comfortable and smug existence, 'fighting' only company battles, can do well to reflect occasionally at the end of a 'stressful' week that we don't really know the true meaning of the word.

Another legacy of all this is the perpetuation for quite a while longer than would otherwise have been the case of the class barriers in business and the civil service – areas left relatively untouched by the great leveller of war service – compared with other walks of life. Meritocracy has had to wait a while. Post-war Britain may have slung out the old-style Tory party and brought in the most radical prime minister of the century in Clem Attlee, but it inherited a top management infrastructure of people unchanged in background, training and attitudes since the 1930s, people whose shortcomings would be comfortably hidden for more than a decade to come behind protected Empire and Commonwealth markets and world shortages of most things we made. They never had it so good.

Whatever the reasons, complacency, lack of vision and small 'c' conservatism have bequeathed to British industry a lot of chairmen and MDs who, if the clock could be rolled back, would not even be thought worth employing by their more dynamic, thrusting younger board members.

I labour the point because it seems to me to be so important in understanding some of the obstacles which most companies need to tackle to a greater or lesser degree. An organisation takes its lead in terms of company style and culture from the man or woman at the top. If they are aloof, lacking in vision and commitment, closed to new ideas and out of touch with the market place of today and tomorrow – then that is what that organisation is about.

The goods news is that the three score and ten rule is rapidly resolving the problem. But almost as bad have been some of the top management styles which have followed. A whole generation of young management trainees cut their teeth on the fictional morals and ethics of Joe Lambton in *Room at the Top*, on the Ian Fleming–James Bond karate-chop approach to leadership, and on the character who has fashioned more managers than all our business schools put together, the late Patrick Wymark as John Wilder in *The Plane Makers* and then *The Power Game* series on television. Machiavelli's 'Prince' was even required reading when I was at business college. 'Old Nick', as we have seen, has had a bad press over the centuries, his christian and surnames both now synonymous with all kinds of nastiness. The main modern management lesson – perhaps the only one – from his writings and action, however, was his conviction that mercenary troops were responsible for the weakness in the Italian states. He argued the need for a citizen army to replace them. There are useful parallels here for business. The citizen army is loyal and mutually self-interested in the success of defending their town/organisation, and of furthering its interests. Mercenary armies have loyalties only to themselves and what's in it for them. You can spot these parallels within some companies, particularly turnaround companies, where a management equivalent of 'The Magnificent Seven' team of gunslingers, from heavens knows what backgrounds, has been brought in to sort things out. Alright in the short term, but remember Niccolò Machiavelli's warning if the outsiders never really make the effort to become insiders, teamworkers.

Pulling strokes, wheeling and dealing, playing company politics, bedding bosses wives and 'Machiavellian' plotting all became apparently the fashionable way to behave as a 'top businessman'. Television soap operas set in the business world keep these values alive. It can work for a period, and it is true that wheelers and dealers can generate irrational loyalty and affection from some of their people – lovable rogues. But it is no way to run an enterprise which has a future. That we can today contemplate behaviour like this as an acceptable even desirable means of conducting business life is alarming. One of the reasons, I think, is the separation of working life from domestic life which flowed from the industrial revolution and the division of labour. In the old days, when cottage industries were more the norm, work and domestic morals were one and the same. Visit Florence today and you can still find artisans' houses with the workshop on the street level and the living quarters above. A Florentine potter, carpenter or baker cannot divorce business and domestic morals; he is living with his family above and within the business. Put that carpenter or baker however in a factory fifteen miles away, for eight hours a day, working with people who do not live near him and have no contact with his family, and he becomes a different person. Dual standards of behaviour and morality are not just possible, but likely.

What of our hard-pressed business executive – working ten hours a day, commuting two, regularly away overnight on business at home and abroad? He can be a hard man at work and a big softy at home, but is it right? And is it any wonder that the pressures this imposes on him can become intolerable? Working women, working mothers, it seems to me, have it even worse. Not only do they have to clear the daily hurdles of sexism to mix it with the best in the scrum of business life, they then also have to somehow create a caring mother figure for their children, throwing the two contrasting worlds into even higher relief.

The explosion in telecommunications, the use of computerised workstations, sophisticated fax and the rest, may one day return us to the concept of village and community life. More and more people should be able to work from home, the wasteful commuting to and from 'the office' may become redundant, city centres may yet die. But that is still some way off and the dual moral standards, the unspoken schizophrenia will continue. Minimise it – but acknowledge its existence. At the moment the good guys generally do not win. Shane died with Alan Ladd.

One of the main preoccupations of any good chief executive should be plans for his or her succession – as that Scottish survey refreshingly showed. Where will the business be ten years after they have moved on or retired? 'Lovable rogues' think of little but themselves. We should perhaps rediscover our eighteenth-century Prussian philosopher Immanuel Kant, rather than Machiavelli. He taught the importance of treating people as an end and not just as a means, distinguishing morality from mere prudence and denying any moral merit to actions not morally motivated. G. E. Moore arrived at similar conclusions from another starting point, arguing that it is impossible for moral goodness to exist in any action that is not wholly good in itself. These are radical sentiments which could bankrupt a lot of charities, but save the Queen from the embarrassment of meeting some of the types she currently must to dish out gongs twice a year.

Kant was in many ways a strange man to have brought to us some of the theories he did. Stunted from a deformity from birth, hollow-chested, he led a lonely, pecunious existence in Königsberg. Like Newton, who he greatly admired, it is thought that he never made love. I think this may be the secret of many great men of art and philosophy. All their sexual energies become sublimated to their work. On the American summer camp I mentioned earlier, I was told after a month that they allegedly put something in the grape juice to stop you thinking about girls (it was an all-boys camp). I didn't know about this until then, but suddenly realised why I'd had so much energy – for ever swimming, canoeing and running like some crazed Japanese game-show contestant. This kind of thing might explain some of the prison riots we read about, although experiments involving the medicine cabinet and the office tea urn are probably unwise, and certainly illegal. Serious parallels there with a Canadian company which was prosecuted in 1985 for releasing a gas, through the office air-conditioning system, designed to make people happy to work harder.

Kant certainly would not have approved. His dictum from *Critique of Practical Reason*, published in 1788, was 'act always to treat humanity, whether in your own person or that of any other, always as an end withal, and never as a means only' and 'There is nothing in the world, or even out of it, which is unqualifiably good but a good will'. Shakespeare in *Hamlet*, writing almost two hundred years earlier, had reached similar views – 'Words without thoughts never to heaven go'.

The abrasive management personality cult is rapidly losing favour and, for all but the smaller or most entrepreneurial businesses, that is a good thing.

Another style of very top management which can be a more unwitting block on progress is that of the specialist, the engineer or the chartered accountant who has been promoted from production director or finance director to the top job. They know what is technically possible and what is affordable respectively, but may not have been sufficiently exposed to the market place to know what is needed of the organisation by its customers. As a result the company may well become production-led, trying to sell what it makes, rather than market-led, making what will sell. It may well become a 'tightly run ship' in terms of budgetary control, risk limitation and exposure, with profit improvements being sought principally from cost cutting, de-manning, de-stocking, tighter credit control, asset sales and rationalisation rather than from improved market share, new product development and the strategic assault on new markets.

Chief executives who lack market-place experience and vision should acquire it or surround themselves with people – executive and non-executive directors – who have, and they should listen and learn. Research by Professor Peter Doyle when at the University of Bradford Management Centre revealed that two-thirds of British firms said they were not good at marketing, and had no clear marketing objectives or competitive strategies.

Comparisons with British managers and Japanese managers working in subsidiaries in Britain highlighted the problem. The Japanese managers principally believed market share and volume brought profit: the British that profit came from rationalising and cost cutting, with market share and volume considerations secondary. The Japanese worked to marketing strategies: the British work to budgets.

A gauge of the seriousness of these weaknesses can be found in any number of gloomy statistics from economists. The UK share of world trade, for example, in the 1960s was around twenty-five per cent for manufactures and twenty per cent for services: they are now around seven per cent and eight per cent respectively. The volume of UK manufactured exports over the six years to 1986 increased by one per cent: imports were up by fifty-five per cent.

It is all very well those Scottish companies and others putting the need to improve their external image high on their priorities, but a dab of powder and rouge will not make the old girl look any better if a real change of face is needed. It is not that many companies are not communicating – the problem is they are communicating perfectly well what they are, and what they are is out of step with what the market now wants. If you are one of those lone voices in a production-led company, getting no support and no understanding from a board dominated by the worst type of accountants, tin-bashers and time-servers, my advice is to get out and find another company where you can really contribute. In my view many companies need a takeover, management buy-out or receivership to create acceptance of the scale of change necessary for some form of regeneration.

## Company Politics

There is a story that internal politics got so bad at the BBC at one time that people started stabbing each other in the front.

Some organisations are riddled with company and departmental politics, diverting obscene percentages of people's time and energies away from the commercial objective. The malaise seems to me to bear little relationship to the size of organisation, but every relationship to the style of leadership and state of morale. Weak or preoccupied leaders and unclear lines of responsibility are the main causes of internal jealousies and resentments, along with over-manning where idle hands and minds can and do make mischief. It is not unusual to find situations so bad that certain people and groups consciously or unconsciously work against each other, seek to undermine the performance of others and rejoice secretly at resultant failures and avoidable mistakes. Picture the scene in an imaginary medium-sized engineering firm in Birmingham, a sub-sidiary of a large holdings company.

The Finance Director is convinced nobody else can read a balance sheet, and that they all think budgeting is some kind of corporate 'Trivial Pursuits' game he plays just to keep himself busy and to snoop on everyone.

The Production Director sees the rest of the management team as an effete bunch of pen-pushers, who have no idea what the real business is about – making 'things' – and who look down their university noses at him for only having a Higher National.

The Personnel Director wishes he could go back to the good old days of actually *hiring* people, instead of all this 'natural wastage'. Keep the indirects down, that's all he hears from upstairs. What's the point of having a personnel director if you don't let him interview people and recruit and stuff like that? Why can't they just start making *more* 'things'?

The Sales Director sees himself and his salesmen as the thin red line out there in the field every day, bringing in the orders that keep the production lot and all the rest in beer and skittles. And he's *really* in touch with the customers. Not like the new young marketing director (the third in two years), who wouldn't know a key account if he fell over one – which he well might one day at the annual trade hospitality booze-up at Twickenham.

The Marketing Director is wondering why he ever came. Of all things, a Midlands tin-bashing company. It wasn't at *all* like this at Unilever. The MD actually asked him what an omnibus was the other day! Probably thinks a TVR is a plastic sports car made in Blackpool. Not that there will ever be the budget for a campaign on the box if the finance director has his way. Oh well, he got the magic title 'director' for the first time. Another year and it won't look too bad on the CV for the next job. Must get back to FMCG – and the *South.*

The Managing Director, a cost accountant by training, just puts up with the lot of them. He knows what he's going to do and if they don't like it, they can lump it. And if that toffee-nosed FCA of a finance director makes one more crack about Cost and Works types, he'll fire him. Anyway, can't wait to take apart his latest end of year accounts. Remember his first lot? Done to some bloody silly ICA exposure draft on inflation accounting. The best laugh he's had since the production director tried to justify some new machine tools he was after with DCF forecasts. Hilarious.

The non-exec Chairman, unknown to everyone, has been patiently trying to flog the place off for the past year to TI, GKN, Imperial Metals, anyone who'd listen to him. Not a hope. Some Kuwaiti syndicate with more money than sense is sniffing, though for reasons he can't fathom. If that falls through, he thinks the best bet would be to wind up the production and sales directors into putting together a management buy-out package – the only two with any idea. From a group point of view that's better City and trade union PR than yet another closure. And it'd also raise a few bob. Best he can do. Half a day a month is all he can spare. Half a day too much as far as he's concerned.

Tackling problems like the mess parodied here at the root – top management – is the only answer, but such is the danger and seriousness of this disease of company politics that it should be known to be a subject for instant dismissal if instances can be proven against individuals and groups.

There are at least three group conditions which affect attitudes and morale: the extent to which people share a common goal; how worthwhile that goal is thought to be; and how achievable the goal appears.

When employees do not recognise the real target for their competitive energies, when it is perhaps too remote or to huge for them to feel they can possibly influence, then they can feel the need to draw their own battle lines around them, to score victories and recruit allies and followers. Change this by ensuring more regular and a clearer understanding of company and departmental objectives and performance, and the results can be dramatic. John Garnett when at The Industrial Society quoted the case of a section of a company employing four hundred men which, principally through systematic briefing, reduced total costs by six per cent and processing costs by twenty per cent. Create a common target – the competition, poor quality, whatever, and if professionally managed, people will respond with a team spirit they will enjoy and from which they can obtain greater job satisfaction and fulfilment. Institutionalise ways to demonstrate to people that they are important, that their contribution is valued, and not insignificant, nor taken for granted. We all need to feel important for our own and group esteem. If we do not get this from a positive role as part of the organisation, we will create one for ourselves – likely as not as a kind of leader of the opposition.

As an example, research has shown that if you conducted this experiment with a largish shop floor, surprising results would follow. Take out a small group of workers and put them in a different, smaller area, and give them an extra tea break. Productivity would go up. Pipe in canned music. Productivity would go up. Give them yet another tea break. Productivity would go up. Then remove all the special privileges. And productivity would go up yet again.

What would be happening would have little to do with perks and privileges. It would be simply that the people felt special, felt that their management was taking a real interest in them, and this could lead to dramatically increased production performances over an experimental period.

## Well Done – Thank You

If the only time you hear 'well done' from your boss is when he or she is ordering a steak, then something is wrong – with your boss or yourself.

A simple 'thank you' or 'well done' can improve morale and performance dramatically. Saying 'well done' twenty per cent more than we currently do will have a tremendous effect. Remember though that most of us know the difference between genuine praise and phoney praise. Also do not just praise and encourage the high achievers. They need it less and would benefit less. Highly motivated, ambitious people know they are going places, and whilst they welcome an informal recognition of this (formal recognition comes in their career progression and pay packets), it will spur them on only marginally more.

It is the regular person who will most value recognition. They know they are not shooting stars in the organisation, either through choice or through limited ability, but they do believe themselves to be diligent, reliable and the people who make any enterprise actually work. Clerical workers, cleaners, post room people, copy typists, telephonists, messengers, security men – they *are* the company in some respects and middle and senior management who pompously forget this are inviting poor morale and company politics. In so many companies recognition of ordinary folk only comes with retirement, or when they leave to take up another job or have a baby. If management would spend as much time praising good work on a routine basis as they do thinking up things to say in those embarrassing speeches at leaving parties, then so much more would be achieved.

Making meaningless leaving party speeches really can be depressing. Much adieu about nothing. I once remember a boss opening up his talk to a gathering of office people (half of whom he barely knew) with the words, 'Making a speech thanking a retiring friend at his leaving party is a bit like making love to a widow. You know it's been done before, and probably very much better . . .' – at which point a recently widowed lady burst into tears and ran out howling.

The point is that in a successful organisation everyone who contributes to that success on a regular, on-going even routine basis is part of a winning team, and by definition a winner themselves. It is not just the chief executive, the supersalesman or the boffin who put the stripe in the toothpaste who are the winners – the whole organisation is the real winner. A regular supporter of a winning football team feels like a winner too, just as much as, and sometimes *more* than the career professionals on the pitch and on the bench. A manager or captain who thanks his supporters in the programme, on a TV interview or over the public address system, is being very shrewd.

If most people are winners in this context, the managers who realise it, walk the floor and acknowledge it, can achieve dramatic and lasting benefits. Effective and popular leaders put into practice this principle. So do good schoolteachers, sports coaches and good parents. Praise and encouragement have also been proven to be important tools in the treatment of children and others with psychological problems, as well as in the rehabilitation of offenders.

The northern European suspicion of anything other than the big stick – or at least the stick and carrot – approach to motivation, however, still leaves many managers, parents and teachers uncomfortable about using too much praise. It is seen as soft or weak. The reality is that the corollary of a management style which is based on encouragement and praise is the very tough expectations it raises amongst bosses and workmates, peer groups, for consistent good work, self-discipline and to not let the side down in any way. Self-policing can be the toughest form of policing of all – there can be no fun in getting away with things, you *know* what makes up a good day's work, and so do those around you. No amount of coming in late, petty pilfering, delicious malicious gossip and bad-mouthing the company is acceptable. You're treated as important, as a winner – and only losers and nobodies behave that way, don't they?

This awareness of the importance of others can profitably be carried over into business and social life outside a work environment. Acknow-ledging the role and importance of others becomes a way of life which can make your own life so much more pleasant and less stressful. If when your barber asks how you want your hair cut you snap back, 'in silence', then don't expect a great haircut. If you don't make any effort with eye contact, body language and common courtesy with shop assistants, bus conductors or bank clerks, then chances are you will be shaving off a little of the joy that can be found in life from others.

It can also backfire rather badly. A friend of mine tells the story of when he waited on table for a while in a top and rather posh hotel restaurant, where the head waiter had something of a reputation for keeping up proprieties. Virtually every other day a local solicitor would use the restaurant for lunching various clients, and each time he was rude and left very mean tips. One day, when the restaurant was especially full, the two men were just leaving when the head waiter bellowed: 'Excuse me, gentlemen. You seem to have left your bus fares on the table.' Other diners burst into laughter and the man never returned.

Hardly great customer relations you might think. But if this chap had been souring the ambience of the restaurant and making his waiters miserable for years, it really was a shrewd move to drive him away. What it also was, of course, was a very big and public 'thank you' to his own staff.

As you can see, it is not true that it costs nothing to say 'thank you'. It costs time and it costs in terms of analysing your nature and recasting it a little if necessary. If by temperament you are more of a loner than a team manager, short-tempered and self-centred, then saying 'thank you' as if you mean it, in a non-contrived 'this is me saying thank you' kind of way, certainly will cost. But the effort is self-evidently worth it.

## None So Deaf . . .

. . . as those who will not hear.

Another common obstacle to communication and business success is the inability of people in authority to listen, and as a result the inability of the enterprise to react to things that customers, the market and its own people are saying.

The Greeks believed that a town ideally should grow no larger than the size of crowd that can hear the voice of one man. There remains a great deal of truth in this because even though we now have microphones, loudspeakers, written media, films, TV, radio and videos, we still miss the point. We have certainly grown into far larger groups that can still hear the voice of one man – but have we yet developed any interactive way permitting us to question that man? That was the point, and it remains just as valid today despite all our smart technology. It need not be a problem in companies, however. Most group sizes permit dialogue – listening as well as speaking.

The problem is that most of us don't want to listen, and the people with whom we think we communicate don't either. Add to this the fact that we only retain about ten per cent of what we are told anyway, and only even understand less than ten per cent of the words in the English language, and the scale of the listening problem becomes clear.

Mary Parker Follet in *Dynamic Administration** is, as ever, well worth reading on this general subject area. The problem is that bosses run the risk day in day out of being deaf to the views and criticisms of subordinates. If he or she is autocratic these views will not be expressed in the first place, and even if not, he or she is the boss, and so is obliged neither to listen nor be sensitive to the views of others around. Real autocrats in any case will have surrounded themselves with people likely to agree with them anyway. You know the type – *'Don't* agree until I've finished discussing this with you!'

Some knowledge of the psychological barriers can help us towards an understanding of our own shortcomings, and through that to those of others and how to cope with them.

The suggestion that we should listen to someone in a work environment may well be met with resistance because we tend to feel most comfortable with a status quo. We are all generally suspicious and resistant to change which new information may herald. Also, if we have a shrewd idea that the topic of the communication is something we feel strongly about, then there is even less likelihood of our agreeing to listen to arguments or counter-arguments. After all, it is a subject upon which we have already deliberated and reached a public or private conclusion which satisfies us.

The chances are we will not listen, but anticipate what is being said and go on to a kind of mental auto-pilot, nodding and 'humphing' until we can butt in and give our own views. It is probable that this unwelcome interruption will not be listened to either, and the other party will simply bide time waiting for a cue to grab the conversation back, at which point we switch off, go back onto auto-pilot, and so on. We can all think of subjects on which we admittedly have closed minds. Although I would happily bring in the birch for people who park in my

*Pitman, London, 1965

space, I am implacably opposed to the reintroduction of hanging, and no amount of persuasion, facts and figures are likely to sway me. It's rather like discussing politics or religion with committed people.

If we find our views being challenged, or worse still feel we are being criticised in some implied or explicit way, then we have more than boredom to cope with. Frustration may arise, characterised by aggression, regression, fixation and resignation – all states capable of being experimentally induced in clinical conditions. All of this will certainly make effective communication near impossible. Aggression, apart from the obvious risk of physical attack, can include throwing things, verbal abuse, slamming doors, kicking wastebins, or self-inflicted injuries like punching the wall. Regression can lead to juvenile behaviour – crying, telling tales, sulking and pouting perhaps, going back to childhood escapes which may then have worked.

Fixation is where the person cannot concentrate on the subject under review and instead some act or gesture is repeated again and again, even though he or she knows it will accomplish nothing – Lady Macbeth washing her hands time and time again to get rid of imagined blood stains is a good example of a fixation. Pipe-smokers may scrape their pipe-bowl noisily with a penknife, others may persistently smooth their hair back; a frustrated housewife may develop a fixation about dusting, cleaning, bathing the children, tidying cushions, and so on. It was alleged that millionaire Howard Hughes became obsessed with the need to avoid germs and diseases. Even more serious can be the state of 'resignation' sometimes found amongst the homeless or the unemployed, people who have simply given up. A typical resigned response in a commercial situation might be: 'I've put up with this place for twenty years, nothing will ever change'. People in this state of mind spread depression and will no longer try to make things better.

Try and spot any of these traits in yourself and others around you. Employees in these states of mind can become highly susceptible to being led and organised by other malcontents. If things get really bad the better people and customers of course simply go elsewhere, if they can. If situations do reach an extreme, then it is wise to create a set of circumstances for yourself or for others in which people can express their frustration without subsequent embarrassment or criticism. Criticism never really works because we either do not accept that we are in the wrong at all, or resent having our noses rubbed in our more obvious mistakes. Let them blow off steam. This is known as catharsis and is a basic form of therapy. Talking to a trained counsellor or company friend, or writing down your annoyances, can make you feel so much better, and help you put things into perspective. Some American companies hold 'rap sessions', where management or supervisors make themselves available to employees who can sound off about things if they want to, and generally tell them how things ought to be run. Hitting strawmen with big sticks, I suggest, should be left to the Japanese.

The real solution is to create the kind of environment in which morale is high, people are interested and committed, and in which regular short, factual, two-way communication is expected and welcome.

If bosses'won't listen, if the board seems deaf to new ideas, then it can often help to have respected outside third parties make the case for you – perhaps a leading management consultancy firm, a market research de-brief by the agency, or even one or two customers friendly to you passing remarks. Then it can become *their* idea, *their* views, not just a reluctant acceptance of something from a subordinate which, by implication, they should have realised themselves. A window on the outside world may be necessary to cast fresh light.

Top management is subject to frustration, even to the point of regression, as much as anybody and more than most. Symptoms include difficulty in making apparently routine judgements, reluctance to delegate, becoming very thin-skinned, and developing irrational fix-ations with routine trivia, like expenses sheets or bad timekeeping. Meanwhile the strategic issues go unaddressed, they begin to speak in broad generalisations without relating them to specific issues where decisions are required, and they develop irrational support for certain people and points of view. The loss of judgement and inability to make distinctions obvious to others is one sign that they may have regressed. Another is uncritical suggestibility. So is a longing to return to the familiar past as a place of refuge, accompanied by an unwillingness to face the future, change. The 'good old days' and previous, now-retired or deceased managers and directors can be elevated to rose-tinted perfection, their likes and qualities never to be met again.

The relief from whatever pressures are causing the problems is the rather obvious best solution, if they are known and actionable. If not, catharsis with the help of his or her immediate peer group – a problem aired and shared and all that – should help, as would counselling and role-playing if circumstances could be created to make them accessible, perhaps on a suitable residential senior management course.

Should you really believe your boss to be in such a state of regression as to need psychiatric help, telling him would not be a wise career move. And remember that our own reactions to people suffering from different levels of frustration may not be entirely rational either. We may become hostile and so make the situation even worse. The temptation is to misjudge their symptoms and treat the people as useless and awkward. Quite a vicious circle.

The next time you find yourself getting steamed up about something, consider whether your judgement has become irrational because of frustration: consider the possibility that you might after all be wrong. Blaming others, the creation of scapegoats is a classic and dangerous feature of frustration. At one extreme, a study reported in the USA in 1940 showed a strong correlation between the number of people lynched – negroes mainly – and the price of cotton (Minor [sic] Studies in

Aggression: VI Correlations of Lynchings with Economic Indices' by C. I. Hovland and R. R. Sears, the *Journal of Psychology*). In a more general sense blaming the boss, blaming assistants, blaming production, blaming component suppliers . . . is a good telltale warning to ourselves to stand back and reassess whether that is the real truth. Again, we must work to know ourselves.

The following checklist is a good way to assess yourself as we close this personal section of the book. It was prepared by American management expert Gerald M. Phillips from suggestions made by various executives. It appears in his excellent and highly readable book, *Communicating in Organizations*\*, and I have amended it very slightly for British consumption.

Items on the checklist represent criteria for getting on in an executive capacity. Those marked with an asterisk are criteria in which ability to communicate effectively plays an important role. Where you honestly believe you are up to standard, give yourself a tick. On the starred items, give yourself two ticks. Score twenty-five ticks or more and you are shaping up well for an executive career.

## Job Performance

*Tick*

_____ 1. Performs job as described in the job description without making mistakes

_____ 2. Performs the job on time

_____ 3. *Calls the attention of immediate superior to legitimate problems in performing the job and asks guidance if necessary

_____ 4. *Draws attention of immediate superior to problems with other people's work in such a way that unobtrusive corrections are possible

_____ 5. Avoids talking about personal problems with immediate superiors

_____ 6. Suggests ways to improve and make more effective his or her job as described in the job description

_____ 7. *Convinces superiors of ways to save money or speed up work

_____ 8. Avoids conflict with associates over work

_____ 9. *Is able to settle disputes between colleagues

_____ 10. *Collaborates with others to solve problems

## Personal Style

_____ 1. Dresses appropriately for the job

_____ 2. Does not advertise sexuality

\*Macmillan, New York, 1982

\_\_\_\_ 3. *Does not conduct personal business on the premises
\_\_\_\_ 4. Speaks well of colleagues and the organisation
\_\_\_\_ 5. ·Does not gossip
\_\_\_\_ 6. Does not spread rumours
\_\_\_\_ 7. Does not belong to a political faction in a work sense
\_\_\_\_ 8. Associates generally with the people around him or her
\_\_\_\_ 9. Does not socialise intensely with work colleagues
\_\_\_\_ 10. Supports the organisation's ancillary efforts like charity appeals

## Communications Skills at Work

\_\_\_\_ 1. Asks useful questions
\_\_\_\_ 2. Answers questions clearly and concisely
\_\_\_\_ 3. Passes on information accurately
\_\_\_\_ 4. *Works effectively in problem solving in small groups
\_\_\_\_ 5. *Defends opinions with evidence
\_\_\_\_ 6. *Makes effective public presentations
\_\_\_\_ 7. Encourages others to work effectively
\_\_\_\_ 8. Shows an understanding of the organisation's objectives
\_\_\_\_ 9. Does not patronise, indulge or insult others
\_\_\_\_ 10. Makes complaints that are justified
\_\_\_\_ TOTAL

Now repeat the exercise and mark honestly how you think your immediate superior would have marked you. The difference between the two will be some indication of the extent to which you need to improve your communication in that direction.

If you feel you are getting to know yourself a little better, time now to get to know your organisation and its products or services just as well. They need to communicate too.

# PART TWO
## Corporate Personalities

# Willkommen, Bienvenu, Welcome . . .

So far we have concentrated on you as an individual, swimming with or against the organisational tide. We now look at the corporate you, you as the influencer and shaper of your organisation's personality.

Organisations – companies, local authorities, charities, even family units – do have personalities. Some are friendly and welcoming, efficient yet approachable, others are not. The hand of someone thinking ahead can be seen in most successful organisations. Some shops have signs on the door saying 'No Dogs Allowed', others have signs that say 'Guide Dogs Only'. That's not just somebody's bright idea. It is the natural consequence of an organisation which has a culture set from the top that puts customers first.

Public relations is not an end in itself; it is a lubricant which helps make the entire organisation work more smoothly, with the minimum friction and risk of breakdown. Business success, by its many criteria, will depend in part on the extent to which public relations considerations have been integrated into the organisation's every activity. Everyone should whistle the same tune.

When customers buy a product, they are not generally buying it from a group of individuals, they are buying it from a corporate entity. That corporation may be synonymous with the product, or it may be a general supplier of many things, but that entity exists in their minds. Views will be held about it. It will be seen as efficient/inefficient, reliable/unreliable, modern/old-fashioned, up-and-coming/on the slide, caring/uncaring, and so on.

Customers and potential customers, employees and potential employees, shareholders and potential shareholders will all hold views about your organisation and products. You are communicating with them all the time simply by existing, trading and employing. You are 'doing public relations' of a sort whether you realise it or not. The real question of course is whether you plan and manage your communications, whether you manage the impression and experience that people vital to your success take from you. Expressed in these terms it becomes clear that PR, however it is described and approached, is not a delete option for responsible management. Of course you must manage what you are, and manage what you seem.

# Springtime for Hitler and Germany

Before launching wholeheartedly into a hundred and one ways in which PR can help, some pretty fundamental questions need airing. If PR is so important, why is it that some companies and some products appear to have little if any PR support and still do well? Further, why is it that some suppliers appear to have terrible image problems yet still outsell the rest?

One of my favourite films is *The Producers*, starring the late Zero Mostel and Gene Wilder. In it, in order to make money by a method too complicated to touch on here, they stage a musical in New York in such deliberate bad taste that they feel sure the show will be panned by critics, and close the next day. The hit song in the show is a kitsch little number – 'Springtime for Hitler and Germany' – performed by highly theatrical jack-booted Nazis behaving more like the Television Toppers. In fact, the show is a great hit and our heroes face ruin.

There are some more serious real-life parallels. If image and PR are so important, what went right with Germany and Japan after the war? Virtually before our Tommies were out of their de-mob suits, and throughout Attlee's, Churchill's and Macmillan's 1950s, German and Japanese cameras, electrical goods and the rest began flooding into the shops. My father was with the 11th Armoured Division, the troops that first entered Bergen Belsen concentration camp under a five-day truce towards the end of the war, in April 1945. This was some days before the camera crews arrived to shoot the harrowing footage that now haunts our memories. He tells me that by the time the filming took place the camp had been tidied significantly. The mind can only shrink from the thought of what it was really like on those first few days, and of course before. He will not talk about it. Yet two of his most prized consumer luxuries in the years after the war, along with thousands of other people, were a Volkswagen Beetle and a Grundig tape recorder. At the same time Japanese transistor radios and later TVs, hi-fis and cars have also swamped our home industries.

If PR is so important, how can this have been possible? Surely the image of the Germans and Japanese could scarcely have been worse in the decade to 1955.

The principal reason, admittedly amongst a host of other factors, is, in my opinion, the ironic one that the war had in important respects given both German and Japanese industry and technology a very *good* image worldwide. The efficiency and might, for example, of the German forces, the quality of their ships, aircraft, tanks and artillery, not to mention their early lead in rocket technology, were quite enough to convince anyone that the VW, the people's car, would be second to none in terms of rude, rugged efficiency. And it was. A country whose transmitters could beam in the voice of Lord Haw Haw – 'Germany calling' – could surely build the best reel-to-reel tape recorders. And it did.

Then there are some British companies over the last twenty years who have had very high profile, charismatic leaders, bursting with PR flair – John Bloom, Cyril Lord, Bernie Cornfeld, Sir Freddie Laker, Sir Clive Sinclair – but have their companies benefited by it in the medium term? On the other hand, there have been immensely successful companies whose leaders seemed to have shunned rather than courted personal publicity – Lord Weinstock, 'Tiny' Rowlands, Sir John Clark, the Woolfsons. Not for them the TV chat shows, nor colour supplement features. Another apparent paradox. Or is it?

The fact is that the Blooms, Lakers and Sinclairs all benefited tremendously and directly from public relations, with quite massive publicity creating awareness and warmth for their products and services that would have cost millions in advertising even to approach. The high awareness created certainly drew greater attention to, say, Laker Airways' receivership in February 1981 and to the post-launch controversy over the Sinclair C5 electric vehicle, but the PR scales remained massively in credit, and both Sir Freddie and Sir Clive remain popular national figures.

As for those senior businessmen who seem not to court the limelight, we simply have to be more sophisticated in our definition of publicity. You can be sure that, for instance, Lord Weinstock and Sir John Clark have been very high profile with the audiences who really matter to their businesses – not the man in the street, but to potential British and overseas military and civil customers for GEC's and Plessey's high-tech products. You and I are not in the market, for example, for early warning systems. 'Tiny' Rowlands' Lonhro has huge and varied interests in Africa, and he and his company are certainly well known to the people who place orders and use the firm's services around the world.

Using PR skilfully does not have to mean going for massive national and international consumer publicity, although it might if there are sound commercial benefits to be gained from it – such as for Virgin through Richard Branson, Jaguar Cars through Sir John Egan, the 1985 Band Aid appeal through Bob Geldoff, and indeed the Save the Children Fund through Princess Anne's very active presidency.

The choice does not lie between appearing on BBC's *Any Questions* and a bout of the autistics from the Howard Hughes/Greta Garbo school of PR. The level and nature of a PR campaign simply has to be whatever is appropriate to meet agreed objectives – great, ambitious or modest.

## Whistle a Happy Tune . . .

In most organisations without any clearly defined PR plan, various bits of the task tend to be picked up in the natural course of events by specialist functions – the finance director has to think about the City, shareholders and bankers; personnel and training address recruitment, employee communications, health and safety, and relations with any unions; sales looks after customer relations, with a bit of grudging help from production, R&D, quality control and distribution; the buying department keeps suppliers on their toes; the MD or marketing director will probably be the ones to talk to the trade press and trade associations, and play the occasional googly from the consumer media. As for 'the company image', that is probably taken care of by sales and marketing in trade and in any consumer advertising, in glossy sales brochures, by giving the odd £500 to a local charity, and by nagging the transport manager to keep the lorries nice and clean. Somebody somewhere probably wants to re-design the company logo, notepaper and business cards, but that is on the back-burner as nobody liked the design scamps the local printer's assistant knocked up last year.

If this really is roughly how your face to the world is being managed, then it is easy to see how things can go wrong. Three or four directors, from three or four very different disciplines, are simultaneously the stewards of how your organisation is viewed. Should there be any inter-departmental jealousies or politics the various faces to the world could be so mockingly different as to be self-defeating. At the very least, a corporate spirit and a healthy synergy between departments, the acceptance of common goals, will have been made quite a bit more difficult.

You need to know what the current state of public affairs is before you can plan ahead more constructively. Conducting the kind of crude communications audit described later alongside some independent research is a start, but it needs to lead to a corporate plan. This can feed back to Drucker-style management by objectives, to goal and target setting, more defined management and accountability systems, better budgetary control, better strategic marketing . . . getting everyone to whistle the same tune.

A useful second step, and one to which even the most cynical of MDs can hardly raise objection, is to research and develop a positioning statement.

## Positioning Statements

Art historian Lord Clark maintained that one measurement of civilisation was man's propensity at any given time to design and erect buildings and monuments which would last for many generations. Indeed, in earlier times, these frequently took much longer than the remaining lifetime of the architect and commissioning paymaster even to complete.

I believe that one measurement of the health of a company or other organisation is the propensity of its leaders – the board – to set a corporate strategy for a decade and beyond. Successful world marketing demands nothing less, as the Japanese demonstrate in so many fields and as the best Western companies also show – IBM, ICI and others. Their board's vision is fixed squarely on the middle distance, leaving operational responsibilities in the hands of divisional boards and senior line management. This attitude, typical in multi-nationals, is no less relevant to small and medium-sized companies, and a positioning statement can help raise the sights.

The theory of positioning relies upon an understanding of customer purchase behaviour, and the current and anticipated socio-economic developments in the domestic and international scene. It is a formalised method of first recognising and then managing the way in which customers and others view suppliers of goods and services, and which as a result affects their purchasing decisions.

Most customers carry around with them a view of, or opinion on, organisations and suppliers of importance to them as part of common knowledge. It may be a bit vague and ill-defined. You will have an opinion of some sort on Woolworth stores or Birds Eye frozen foods, for example. This perception will vary with educational standard, sex, background, class, age, ethnic and other factors. Divorced people, as we have seen, can be more cynical than most. When a purchase is imminent, the blurred perception will be brought into sharper focus because the consumer is now becoming more interested, closer to having to come to a decision. The consumer's impression of the organisation and/or its product will encompass both emotional and rational factors when balancing up the 'offer'. When the decision is eventually made, the customer will have unwittingly weighed up in his or her mind the range of emotional perceptions against the physical, tangible factors such as price and availability.

Research has shown just how important emotional factors are in many purchase decisions, especially in service industries where interface with people is likely. Indeed, they often outweigh rational assessment, although on probing this is not normally admitted – post-rationalisation based on physical factors will come into play.

Consumer perception is influenced by many things, such as word of mouth from friends, relatives, TV, radio, magazine and press comment (that is by public relations), by advertising and by point of sale and pack design. With ever-increasing competition, it is the clear, consistent, appropriate and cohesive message that will succeed as the consumer's memory bank retrieves all the data which it has consciously taken in and subliminally been fed. Some element of uniqueness is clearly of great benefit at this stage to prompt appropriate recall.

The positioning of many if not most companies and some products within the market place has occurred quite unwittingly, but those companies which have adopted a clear and long-term business philosophy and style – such as the leading retail chains and supermarkets, and most of the grocery and detergent brands – have generally reaped the benefits in terms of growth, profitability, acceptance of new products/lines and recruitment of the best people.

Positioning requires commitment from the main board to the switchboard over a long period, and the determination, training and management procedures necessary to ensure that the reality will live up to the aspirations being set. Advertising alone cannot achieve the desired results, and if it is dissonant with the reality of the brand or company, if it is too aspirational, then great damage can result. Good advertising can lead by a small distance, and can encourage employees to aspire to higher standards without disappointing customers who find the gap yawning much too widely. The banks, building societies and airlines often get it right. Nationalised industries, by comparison, have frequently over-promised.

Think through a structure for a positioning statement for your own organisation. Start by listing the main socio-economic factors you can see that might affect the demand for your products or services over the next ten years – these may be the demographic trends towards an older population, UK and world trade assumptions, the economic cycle, possible technological developments, changing distribution/retail patterns, the growth of new, low cost competitors, perhaps from the Third World or Pacific Basin, and so on. Separate them into broadly good influences and trends, and bad.

Next, using any research you have and any you can buy off the shelf, briefly describe how you imagine your customers currently know you and your main competitors, and look for any gaps in the offer you are all making which could be exploited, and any areas of profitable, synergistic, diversification which would capitalise on your current strengths.

Finally, attempt to write out a description of where you would like to see the organisation in ten years' time in terms of what it is supplying, to whom and how, and with what propositions – always understanding the implications this has for capital employed, premises, staff and training. If it helps, develop a number of options, some more radical than others.

Many organisations when first tackling the job of positioning appoint a small working party from different disciplines to collaborate and prepare a first draft – perhaps a thousand words would be the maximum you should aim for. Then ruthlessly sub it down to about 200–300 words. The shorter the better. Once the arguments and agonies are over, it will be an invaluable document for use throughout the organisation in various forms, and should become the touchstone, influencing judgements on the variety of opportunist or strategic decisions which arise each month and year – 'does it fit the positioning?' will become as common a question as 'are we living up to the positioning?'

Finding out, researching what the customer wants, having a plan of how to supply it and giving the customers what they want – our consistent theme – attracting them into your club, having them post-rationalise why they choose you, defending their decision, and wearing your 'badge' with pride; this is what positioning at its best can achieve.

# The Corporate Personality

We can make well-known organisations seem like people if we use a little imagination. They do have personalities much like individuals. The point of contact for most with companies or organisations like town halls, DHSS offices and the rest is through the offering or use of its products or services, and through the counter clerks, agents or sales force. Clearly these should all be in tune with the positioning statement you will have developed. There are a number of other points of contact which consumers or business-to-business customers may have – visiting the building, receiving letters and literature, and contact with the switchboard and through it different departments, such as customer relations/complaints. All these should also whistle the same tune.

## People

An internal communications plan soon becomes necessary and your positioning statement provides an excellent reason to look afresh at how internal relations are handled – the noticeboards, house journals, circulars and the rest.

Quite an industry has developed to help mainly larger organisations point everybody in the same direction. British Airways, for example, took more than a year to put all its customer contact staff through a two-day course, led by consultants, designed to help them put people first. Importantly, the initiative had the overt support of the airline's chief executive. Consistently good customer relations and clear market orientation are vital in people businesses such as airlines, hotels and car hire firms. Parallel with this 'people first' drive in the service industries has been the development of quality improvement initiatives in both service and manufacturing industries, generally known as quality circles. Dramatic improvements have been achieved, not just in customer satisfaction and quality control, but in company morale, job satisfaction, lower absenteeism and labour turnover. Glittering prizes. It gives everyone in the group the chance to make an input and to influence decisions taken. There is more than a hint of the Japanese-style participative approach in quality circles, and that is no bad thing. Our cultures are very different but there is much that Western management is already learning from Japan – some of it very similar in style to some of the Scandinavian car companies' work on quality groups decades ago.

Well-ordered common sense is at the heart of the 'people first', quality circle and the briefing group/team briefing initiatives which can benefit organisations of all sizes. When described rather than experienced, each can seem facile and just a consultant's fancy name to jargonise what you probably think you do in your own way already. Unless you are a pretty dreadful organisation there is a measure of truth in this, but marginal improvements can repay themselves time over time. And remember the example given earlier where productivity improved when a group of workers were given extra perks, and improved still further when they were taken away? The very act of senior management involving themselves in, and endorsing, people initiatives like this itself can have an immediate benefit.

## Pointing Everyone in the Same Direction

Briefing groups, now called team briefings, are the best known method in the UK for installing organisational procedures to improve and encourage the flow of information down the line, to help point everyone in the same direction. They were introduced largely through the tireless dedication of John Garnett during his twenty-four years at the Industrial Society – a body which, with the support of management and trade union leaders, primarily exists to promote the fullest involvement of people in their work.

Team briefings have evolved differently in different organisations. In essence it is a mechanism to ensure that management effectively puts over what it *needs* employees to understand. The emphasis on the word 'need' is important. If senior management accepts this need, then the communications process – briefing groups, whatever – becomes an essential duty for management down the line; not something they do half-heartedly when they feel like it. The fact is that most people do not enjoy leading briefings, and will avoid it if they can. Management has to make it very clear that, following training, this is a new, regular and measurable part of their responsibilities, and that failure will be noticed and acted upon.

Team briefing only works if it is frequent and regular – at very least monthly, but better still weekly. It can even be daily for just five minutes. The group has to be led by someone who is clearly accountable for the results of the people brought together – the buck stops with him or her. The size of group is less important than the obvious relevance of the group to meeting these results. It should be held near the place of work – anywhere where you can be heard, and at the 'least worst' time during the working day. The maximum time for a briefing should be 10–15 minutes – people cannot generally absorb more than 7–8 minutes of information at any one time – and less if held as regularly as weekly or daily.

The topics that should be covered are simply those which people in the group need to know about – how well the group is doing in terms of progress; localised issues which can be actioned, such as quality control, machine downtime, safety, administrative support, support from other departments, etc; company policy in a wider sense in so far as it affects the group's work or well-being – new or amended product lines, new plant and machinery, etc; and people issues such as updates on pay and conditions of employment, including any relevant industrial relations issues, which should not be abdicated as so often at present to trade union channels.

Questions should be taken on the issues relevant to the group, mainly as a means of clarification. They are not consultative meetings, however, where decisions and policies can be debated.

The main information covered should be generated by the team leader. Briefing groups are not just a system to pass down the line top management's decisions and views. Information exercising those at the top is, in any case, generally not very relevant to those at the bottom. Instead, the team leader should *tell* his own boss in advance what he or she is covering, and ask for any *relevant* information which should also be passed down. The team leader should also include in the briefings some hard figures on issues like production targets and those detailed above, which can make possible some form of historic measurement of results arising from previous briefings.

One of the biggest obstacles to introducing team briefing systems into organisations can be the attitude of some senior management. They simply do not believe that their junior management and supervisors can perform in this way. Often this can be overcome by a greater degree of self-belief from the very top. When at British Leyland, Sir Michael Edwardes used to have a picture over his desk of two albatrosses flying over the sea, with the caption 'They can because they think they can'. Aviation experts also tell us that in theory bumble-bees ought not to be able to fly – but they do.

On the other hand, the truth may be that some of your people really are not right for this style of management – not having been recruited with this in mind. If so, steps have to be taken to either train people up or remove them. The time has long past in successful organisations when they debated whether they had time to communicate, least of all during valuable company time. Nissan in the UK, for instance, have their supervisors talk for five minutes at the start of each day. When they were recruiting they knew they simply had to take on the right people – operatives and managers. Given the scale of their investment they did not want negative people around. One way they succeeded was to invite people they were considering to take tea, to see their social, inter-personal skills – this was after numeracy, literacy and dexterity testing.

If you do not have the benefit of a green-field site situation, then there is no alternative than to put your existing managers and supervisors through some hoop which will weed out people lacking in the necessary skills and motivation. Business has become far too competitive for any organisation to continue to employ malcontents and grumblers.

# Measurement

If the main objective of team briefings and the like is to let people know how they and their immediate working group are doing, it raises the question of measurement. If someone socially asks how are you, a fair reply is 'compared with what'.

How do we really know how we are doing? I used to be a production manager in a large clothing group manufacturing sweaters, mainly for Marks and Spencer. All of us junior managers were kept very much on our toes by the factory director, who used to walk the job several times a day, asking us how many dozen we had got out so far against target. It worked well, because woe betide anyone who either did not know, or could not at least make an accurate guess to the nearest 50–100 dozen. The story went around, probably more legend than fact, of a young production manager involved in getting out some 3,000 dozen fully-fashioned sweaters a week, who, when challenged on a Tuesday morning for his production figures, nervously spluttered "undreds'.

Those were happy days when management authority could be play-acted with a bank of stop-watches or a slide rule. We worked on a form of piece-work where jobs were based on SAMs, standard allowed minutes. It was marvellous to be able to wave the magic slide rule and tell operatives at any time exactly how much they had earned so far that week. This was in the days before calculators robbed those of us who were slide-rule snobs of all our mystery. I still use one occasionally, however, just to annoy people.

Today, there can be a lot of confusion about just what the target is. For an individual, a group target may not motivate very much. He or she will be pleased if the group hits or exceeds it, but a group target will work at its best only when translated into *tasks* which he or she can relate to and control. It is rather like simply telling a soccer team to go out and win by two clear goals. What the manager and coach have to do is work with individuals on their own weaknesses and duties in the match, as well as engendering a positive team spirit. Just so in, say, a production unit, where the tasks of some operatives may be to slow down and improve quality, others to speed up and maintain quality, others to be more flexible in taking on new lines/jobs, others to reduce absenteeism, others to reduce wastage, and so on.

Numbers – production figures, quality control figures and the rest – are clearly important (not least often for payment purposes), but you cannot talk to people simply about numbers. You have to relate the numbers to tasks. Most junior and supervisory management has to deal in numbers (budgets, sales targets, labour turnover figures, etc). They are the foodstuff of the computers, the number crunchers and our trained alsatians. But at the point of contact with the human end of these figures, the manager has to relate them to very practical issues – like complaints by one operative on piece-work that their machine is older than others and leads to slower working/more downtime/quality problems. No amount of corporate spirit will change this very pragmatic problem – only the manager can. You constantly have to review what people are actually doing, and how they go about achieving defined tasks. Trying to manage just by historic numbers is like steering a ship by the wake. As Edmund Burke said, you can never plan the future by the past.

This means walking the job, regularly walking around the unit for which you are responsible, not sitting in an office or just liaising with people you like or with whom you feel most at ease. One sign of a more responsive, motivated organisation is when managers start talking together face to face or on the telephone about problems, instead of sending memos, copied around the place.

Table One is a useful checklist for running a team briefing or similar group. It helps prepare the team leader and structures the session. Work across the top headings – add to them if you wish – and, for example, report/comment on *quality* in terms of progress (how well the group is doing); policy (this raises broader issues such as new key supplier requirements, new plant and machinery, etc); people (are there any obstacles, are there shortages of staff leading to bottlenecks?); and points for action (maybe more training, better support from QA, other departments, components suppliers, better lighting, ergonomics, etc).

**TABLE ONE**

|  | Quality | Quantity | Time | Cost |
|---|---|---|---|---|
| **PROGRESS** |  |  |  |  |
| **POLICY** |  |  |  |  |
| **PEOPLE** |  |  |  |  |
| **POINTS FOR ACTION** |  |  |  |  |

The ability effectively to manage the performance of others of course has as a prerequisite the need for you, the manager, to be able to manage your own tasks well. And this can still be done by individual managers in organisations where overall the company culture remains in the communications dark ages.

I would suggest that you tailor-make your own version of the following ten-point Personal Performance Review System.

1. Define, redefine if necessary and simplify if at all possible the management structure within your area of responsibility.

2. Make sure you know, and that others know, who is accountable for what tasks, and to whom.

3. Draw up your own Game Plan, as illustrated in Table Two.

    This necessitates your identifying and listing task areas down the left-hand column. If you are a production manager, this may entail introducing new products onto the line, which in turn may require training, work study analysis, rate-fixing, a new machine/product flow layout, more staff/less staff, and so on. For a brand manager it might mean introducing a new sales promotion, a money-off say. In turn, this needs feeding in to the packaging design people, production, selling-in to retailers, briefing the sales force, the trade press, the advertising agency, monitoring the success through research, and so on. Then under another task heading the brand manager may be having to organise the sales conference. This will entail fixing dates, finding and booking the venue, briefing an audio-visual company, producing the business and social side of the conference, and all the rest.

    Alongside each detailed task put the initials of who is accountable for making it happen, and alongside that who is his or her boss. Finally, list the year out alongside — most organisations work on weeks one to fifty-two, either on a calendar or financial year basis. Ticks, crosses or different coloured stickers should show when each activity is planned to begin, and when it should be completed.

    The Game Plan should be kept to one sheet of paper, no matter how big. It can cover an entire wall if necessary. Don't make it look too professional by using Letraset; simply write it out in felt tip pen. It is a living, working planner, not a work of art. What it should convey at a glance is who is responsible for what, and how you are all doing on your targets.

4. Use the Game Plan by writing notes to yourself of things you want to raise with people on the various tasks at appropriate times in the future.

Put the notes in envelopes or little plastic folders and stick them on the time-planner chart. Use the Game Plan. Do not rely simply on memory or immediate pressure of work or your key priorities may be lost.

5. Systemise a means to bring people up to date on what is going on – team briefings, or whatever you decide.

6. Make sure you have a method for keeping in touch yourself on a day to day basis. Walk the job, let yourself be seen to be involved at the sharp end. Be accessible. Be seen to be responsible.

7. Establish your own acceptable standards and make people respect them. This means acceptable codes of behaviour covering a whole range of issues like timekeeping, dress, tidiness, grumbling, language, sexism (jokes, girlie calendars, etc), racism, and so on. It is possible to impose your own culture on a group, even if the corporate whole makes no attempt to. We can all recall some of our schoolteachers who, when teaching exactly the same pupils as other teachers, commanded more respect and better behaviour. To borrow from Herman Wouk's *The Caine Mutiny*: there are four ways of doing things on this ship – the right way, the wrong way, the Navy way – and My Way.

8. To achieve this, do it in stages. The Twenty Per Cent Factor. Unless you are in a green-field situation, you risk going over the top and being ridiculed if you suddenly started trying to impose a new culture overnight.

9. Keep things simple.

10. All of this will never work until it becomes a drill. Relentlessly stick to your Game Plan and your methodology, insist others do the same. Only when your people realise they *have* to work this way will they do so. People dislike and resist change. They are, however, generally happy to accept clear direction if it makes sense. Don't discuss it. Implement it. Stick to it. The results, the benefits should soon follow. Almost everything at work is measurable. Your problem is to find the measurement.

**Table Two: THE GAME PLAN**

| Task Area headings | Who's accountable for task? | Who is their boss? | CALENDAR WEEKS (TO 52) | | | | | | | | | | | | | | | | | |
|---|---|---|---|---|---|---|---|---|---|---|---|---|---|---|---|---|---|---|---|---|
| | | | 1 | 2 | 3 | 4 | 5 | 6 | 7 | 8 | 9 | 10 | 11 | 12 | 13 | 14 | 15 | 16 | 17 | 18 | 19→52 |
| 1 | | | | | | | | | | | | | | | | | | | | | |
| 2 | | | | | | | | | | | | | | | | | | | | | |
| 3 | | | | | | | | | | | | | | | | | | | | | |
| 4 | | | | | | | | | | | | | | | | | | | | | |
| 5 | | | | | | | | | | | | | | | | | | | | | |
| 6 | | | | | | | | | | | | | | | | | | | | | |
| 7 | | | | | | | | | | | | | | | | | | | | | |

## Discipline

Briefing people, communicating with them and motivating them is important, but what happens when some fail to meet targets or standards? In the home, office or factory there regularly arise situations where the person in authority has to take action to tick someone off, or worse.

If you have been able successfully to create an environment where social and peer group pressure asserts itself, then your job will be much easier. The most effective form of discipline is self-discipline, where people almost tell themselves off, and need barely a word or raised eyebrow from you. The Japanese have no swearwords like our own equating to sexual acts or bodily functions. Instead, they are more likely to exclaim, '*Machigatta!*' – 'I've made a mistake!'

Acceptance of reasonable group and company rules and standards is key to a feeling of freedom and belonging. To take advantage of communal life requires acceptance and recognition of the rights of others and our own obligations to the group and organisation as a whole. This feeling of shared values is especially important today. The days in the UK when fear of the poorhouse permitted autocracy are long since over, although the 'bridge to engine room' manner I have described is still adopted by some – mostly ex-military people, second or third generation commercial patricians, or self-made people, risk-takers dismissive of those who are not, people with obsessive feelings of proprietorship. In the West, this approach can still work for a few years at a time – as long as it is in the self-interest of the subjugates to put up with it. Some philosophers, however, argue that an act is not truly moral and right unless we are equally free enough to choose not to behave that way. Self-discipline pre-supposes the freedom of choice to behave 'well'.

In order to assert discipline to greatest effect and with the minimum risk of it backfiring on you, there is a virtuous circle to follow.

1. *Ensure that you are really satisfied that you and your organisation have very clearly communicated what you consider to be unacceptable behaviour or attitudes.*

2. *Reassure yourself that your views of unacceptable behaviour and attitudes are fair, reasonable and shared by those around you. Don't kid yourself on this. If you go around saying, 'That's fair, isn't it?' without waiting for or listening to the reply, you will just be generating resentment.*

3. *Make it clear that punishment for breaches is inevitable.*

4. *Never threaten action on which you cannot deliver for physical, legal or trade union reasons.*

5. *Where anything other than a gross breach of discipline occurs, always give warnings, and put them in writing.*

6. *When giving warnings or considering discipline always find out first why the breach has taken place: it may colour your own and your group's view*

*of what punishment, if any, is merited: it may leave the transgressor with some dignity. Always point out the consequences of ignoring the warning.*

7. *Remain calm and firm at all times – not angry, nor informal. It is your office, you as the steward of your organisation's values who is carrying out the interview – not you as a person who feels humiliated, angry, frustrated or let down. Distance yourself. It helps you and them later to keep a good relationship.*

8. *Make punishments neither too harsh nor too lenient, and do not at this stage begin to ask more of them than you demand of anyone else – don't seem vindictive or 'throw the book' at them. Equally do not apologise for handing out punishment. It should seem to the person as a natural consequence of their own behaviour – not of yours.*

9. *Have somebody with you when giving warnings and when disciplining. As management consultant Vincent Nolan has said, when dealing with conflict, ninety per cent of the emotion is about ten per cent of the content. People are not at their most rational in times of stress, their memories can be blank or highly selective, and outside, their account will be believed, as you would never discuss such a private meeting with anyone else, would you?*

## Time management

Of course, it's all very well outsiders saying give yourself more time to plan or think.

Most people believe they don't have the time, their lives already full with too much to do.

It is always easy to fill time and genuinely feel busy. The truth more often than not, however, is that large percentages of that time are being badly used in terms of priorities. Being a busy fool is common enough. We are all tempted to do the easy, pleasant jobs first, and to leave until last the things we least enjoy. To push papers around and not actually do much, to write a letter or memo rather than be more direct through a telephone call. To wait for others to prompt us to do things we know we should do anyway – like the person lying in bed in the mornings thinking, 'If that alarm doesn't go off soon, I'll be late for work'.

Knowing yourself is again the answer. You have to force yourself out of bad tendencies. The best and simplest way to do this is to write on the paper bag in which you bought your Filofax a list of things you have to do that day or that week. Then number them in terms of *real* priority, priority to meeting the organisation's objectives – not your priority as to ease or fun/hate when you complete each task – and at the end of each day or week tick things off, including yourself if you're still taking the comfortable line of least resistance. When the paper bag is covered in your scribbles, buy a pound of sprouts to get another one – it's a lot cheaper.

The extent to which you may like your boss to see you as conspicuously busy is a moot point. There is a lot of truth in the saying: 'If you want a good job doing, ask a busy man'. On the other hand, the most senior people do seem to be much less likely to be pestered by a procession of mini-crises and deadlines. They seem more able to be on time for meetings *and* to have read the papers beforehand. They seem less likely to be constantly interrupted by urgent-must-take telephone calls when you are in their office, and don't have to shoot off trains at the end of business journeys stuffing 10ps in telephone boxes, like some American spinster working ten bandits in a Las Vegas casino.

Take your cue from your immediate boss. If he or she is still in the busy-bee phase, then your appearing a serene picture of orderliness will probably be mistaken at best for your not having enough to do, and at worst as some kind of smart Alec implied criticism of their own ability to manage. If he or she is more senior and/or takes pride in their orderliness, it is likely that your breathless, can't-stop-now routine will be viewed as inexperience or plain incompetence. Once again, reflective responsing will be called for. But whatever presentational style you judge best for your circumstances, efficient time management must underpin it, or your work effectiveness will be a good twenty per cent lower than it need be for the same effort.

## Quality Circles

Quality circles have become popular to the point of trendiness in some areas of business, although like the abominable snowman, I think they are more discussed and written about than actually encountered.

The idea is to bring together various layers of employees who have a direct effect on the quality of work or service produced. The group meets regularly under a discussion group leader (not necessarily the manager of the team), sometimes called the facilitator. A Quality Circle Co-ordinator will orchestrate the various circles for the organisation as a whole. Management consultancy firm PA is one of the leaders in this area.

Under the facilitator, individual groups (generally comprising repre-sentatives of various departments or disciplines) will appraise quality standards and develop practical steps to achieve lasting improvements.

Remarkable results are claimed by the fans of quality circles. Critics say some systems disenfranchise some from joining in, negate the hierarchical way in which most organisations actually work, and argue that team briefings can achieve as much on quality unless there is a real crisis situation in terms of quality control.

## Other Forms of Employee Communication

Face to face contact – be it team briefing or joint consultation – is invariably the best form of contact, but it is not the only way to communicate. Traditional vehicles include noticeboards, house journals, corporate magazines, employees' annual reports, films and videos.

*Noticeboards*
Well-designed, well-sited noticeboards should not be ignored, and will not be ignored. If they are kept up to date and used, they are one of the cheapest and most efficient forms of communication. However if using the noticeboard is everyone's responsibility, then it soon becomes no one's responsibility. One person – preferably someone from personnel – should be appointed 'editor' of the noticeboards; he or she should control what goes up, for how long, and be responsible for keeping up standards.

Some firms allow their people to use the noticeboards to run small ads, to sell cars or find babysitters. I think this is a good idea, but either special noticeboards should be kept for this purpose, or special parts of general noticeboards. Again, all items which people want to put up should go through the 'editor'. A good idea is to pin up press cuttings from the trade or national press each day or week, to let people see what is being said about the firm. If an executive is to be interviewed on TV or radio that evening or the next day, this should be announced so that employees or their families can tune in if they wish.

In the same way, when a new advertising campaign is about to break, the press ad or the TV storyboard should be pinned up along with a simplified media schedule. Any TV ads could be screened on videos in the canteen. Details of perimeter advertising at sports events, or of sponsorships, can also be put up. People get a great deal of pride from seeing their organisation in the media, and like to know in advance that it is happening. It makes them feel special and to be 'in the know' with their friends and family. 'Hey, Dad, look, your firm is sponsoring this rugby match' is no way for employees to find out about such things. It makes them feel foolish and negative.

*House journals*
Corporate magazines, the glossy kind, are now dying out, except in those larger, probably multi-national companies which find them useful for overseas customers, and to keep other parts of the group in the picture on what others are doing.

House journals or newspapers, however, remain popular. Indeed, there is a lively professional organisation called the British Association of Industrial Editors.

At their worst, house journals are so bad as to be pure kitsch. In one company where I used to work, we had a monthly office raffle based around how many pictures of the chairman would appear in the rag.

So many are full of out of focus pictures of people, unknown to most, retiring or getting married, of football or hockey teams taking on local factory opposition, of thinly disguised management exhortations on quality or capitalism, and of pictures of some snooker star grinning with the marketing director at some trade binge. They are strong on trivia and weak on what people really want to hear about – like pay and conditions, the state of the order book, investment plans, and industrial relations issues. Even when printed in newspaper format, so often they look as though they were written a month ago, and could just as easily be read a month later.

The most successful company newspapers are those which have a clear job to do, where the workforce is big, scattered and probably working shifts. British Rail, the British Steel Corporation and British Coal each have newspapers with circulations of around 215,000, 54,000 and 180,000 respectively. They appear monthly.

I think it is the frequency of appearance which is the key to successful house newspapers, just as much as tight, professional editorial support. We have come to expect news daily, yet most house journals can only appeal monthly, bi-monthly or quarterly, for budgetary reasons, and because there is simply not enough news and interesting features to fill them more regularly.

Even within large conglomerates, where there probably is on the surface plenty of news, the fact is that people mainly want information which is of direct relevance to themselves.

My own view is that too many house journals exist because they are there, and that some elementary readership research would probably shock and depress the management considerably. I'm not really a fan – unless there is a clear objective to be met as with, say, 'Coal News'.

One tactic which can be adopted is to send house journals direct to employees' homes. This hopefully ensures that it stands a better chance of being read rather than scanned and dumped, it involves family and possibly neighbours in the employee's business and, in times of industrial disputes, it can leave open a direct form of communication from management to the employee and his or her spouse, without the seemingly provocative move of by-passing normal joint consultative machinery. Another benefit is that the paper is likely to be read in a less cynical ambience at home than amongst workmates.

### Video

Corporate videos, video company magazines, videos on issues can give management the marvellous impression that they are *doing* something. After all, they are, aren't they? They are on the screen, reading auto-cues like a newscaster and they have invested big money in putting in the video players and monitors, and in making the wretched programmes. Too often the only people meeting any real commercial objectives are the very aggressive video production houses.

The line goes something like this. People have now got used to accessing information, news and views from television. The printed media are dead. A professionally made series of videos, up to broadcast standard (it can't be seen to be inferior to a normal TV programme), is the modern way to get your message over to your people.

Large companies like IBM, H. J. Heinz, Ford, British Aerospace and virtually all the clearing banks make extensive use of video in their mix of communications. Some even have their own video production facilities, right through to editing.

Visual aids *do* help support important messages, and broadcast quality video is the ultimate visual aid. In my experience company videos only work well when used as part of a structured briefing process, either on an on-going basis – say monthly with a video magazine/news bulletin – or when there are specific issues which need to be tackled. I have been involved in the communication of major redundancy programmes with large companies where we have trained the line management – those charged with handling the announcements – in the use of a video, and in role-playing subsequent questions and answers. In these circumstances the value of a video message from, say, the chief executive is in ensuring that *all* the groups being informed (some of them on shifts) hear the news in exactly the same way, and do not get embroidered versions of it from line management. It also helps define the line manager's limited autonomy to go beyond what has been said by the boss, and which in any case will be re-emphasised in a take-away printed summary to be distributed at the end. The mixture of video, face to face *and* print was always important. However much bad news may be half expected, it still comes as a shock, and many people take in almost nothing of the details you agonised over in the filming.

Handling redundancies has been a miserable feature of recent business life. My first taste came when I was training officer of a firm which decided to close one of its northern factories. The personnel manager and myself conducted face to face interviews with everyone involved to discuss detailed redundancy payment arrangements and any possibilities of work elsewhere in the group. This followed a flying visit by the chairman to break the news in the canteen. The hardest bit for me was when one of the disabled people plaintively thanked me for keeping her on as long as we had anyway. This was a single person in her fifties, still supporting her mother. Leaner and fitter and all that . . .

Ironically, video briefings in situations like this are better, more personal and more caring than a gauche bit of canteen oratory by some remote top boss. He or she can be on video, well coached, to add weight, but the people sharing the impact with you are your direct manager and your peer group. It also minimises the risk of industrial action and rabble-rousing by either shop stewards or other articulate workforce people, who are generally more skilled and experienced in mass meeting tactics than top business people.

Given clear objectives and a trained team of group leaders, video can be a very powerful tool. Given woolly objectives, a desire to *use* all that equipment you have put in and to *do* something with all the TV training you have given people, the results will be expensive and will undermine your future more – targeted attempts to use the medium more seriously. Video should be a management tool, not an executive toy.

# Corporate Identity

## Architecture and Interior Design

The culture and tone of voice of an organisation, as we have seen, is one important clue to its personality. Its 'dress sense' – architecture and interior design – is another.

There are many stereotypes of how we expect certain types of office/business building and interiors to look – banks a little dark with mahogany doors, the manager behind a green leather-topped desk; advertising agencies, all glass, chrome, open-plan and potted palms; an engineering company, flat-roofed, low-rise 1950s, with pictures of dour founders on the wall, apprentice-boy pieces in glass cases, and a pervading smell of hot oil wafting in from somewhere – and so on.

Your choice of office building in which you might receive visitors (or your choice to remain in it) will say a lot about you. A good brief to an architect or interior designer will encompass much of what you are striving to achieve in your positioning. Your building will be and remain a deliberate statement of corporate self-expression, and of where you are taking the organisation.

The use of architecture and design in this way of course is not new, and over history it has been taken to some extraordinary lengths – such as at Versailles.

In ancient China in the thirteenth century Kublai Khan had quite a family to feed, and many subjects and visitors to impress. He had four wives, each with their own court of over 300 damsels, plus pages, eunuchs and other attendants amounting to more than 10,000 persons per wife. Venetian trader Marco Polo, then twenty-one, and by any other name one of Khan's key account customers, was clearly impressed by his Imperial supplier when he wrote of the awesome spectacle of the Hall of the Palace, an area which could easily dine 6,000 people. 'The building is altogether so vast, so rich and so beautiful, that no man on earth could design anything superior to it. The outside of the roof also is all colours with vermilion and yellow and green and blue and other hues, which are fixed with a varnish so fine and exquisite that they shine like crystal, and lend a resplendent lustre to the Palace as seen for a great way round.'

If all this has given you a taste for brightening up the directors' dining room, then I suggest you stop short at emulating the next two observations by Marco Polo, for fear of giving your MD ideas above his station . . .

*At every door of the hall (or, indeed, wherever the Emperor may be) there stand a couple of big men like giants, one on each side, armed with staves. Their business is to see that no one steps upon the threshold in entering, and if this does happen, they strip the offender of his clothes, and he must pay a forfeit to have them back again; or in lieu of taking his clothes, they give him a certain number of blows . . .*

*They have the mouth and nose muffled with fine napkins of silk and gold, so that no breath nor odour from their persons should taint the dish or the goblet presented to the Lord. And when he takes the cup all the Barons and the rest of the company drop on their knees and make the deepest obeisance before him, and then the Emperor doth drink. But each time that he does so the whole ceremony is repeated . . .*

Architecture through the ages has generally had a clear objective in mind – commercial, political or religious. Renaissance Florence was shaped by successful merchants like the Medici; Napoleon and Haussmann for their differing reasons left their mark on Paris; Empress Maria-Theresa and Franz-Joseph on Vienna; Mussolini on Rome. The church of course is the real master in the use of architecture and design to meet objectives. Visit Sacré Coeur in Paris, having imagined the surrounding poor neighbourhoods a century or more ago. Then, pretend you are a local Parisian of the eighteenth or nineteenth century living in a candle-lit hovel, and look up at the huge figure of Christ in the dome – eyes staring straight at you, arms ready to embrace you. As for St Peter's . . .

Business architecture has changed dramatically in recent years, however. Look at the Victorian bank buildings, or more particularly at the pension and assurance buildings in the major cities of London, Manchester, Newcastle, Glasgow, and the rest. They look like great cathedralesque edifices that may not have pleased Kenneth Clark's eye, but would have told him something about their confidence and civilisation. It is clear that the brief for the Victorian architects was to create buildings which would reassure ordinary people first that if their money was inside it was impregnably guarded, and secondly that these organisations taking your shillings and pence for retirement pensions and rainy days would actually be around when you came to collect it. They were literally built to last. The *Building Chronicle* in the mid-nineteenth century remarked that classical architecture suited banks, since it denoted 'a sentiment of enduring strength and close security, a manner which may signify a solid and confident substantiality'.

The needs of the market are now very different. People do not need reassuring that the banks and pension companies have got their money safely locked away, nor that they are going to be around in fifty years. That is taken for granted. What customers now expect is for their financial institutions to be modern, high-tech, on the ball and bustling with bright young people and computers. This has led us to the NatWest Tower, the new Stock Exchange and the flimsy looking glass tower-blocks of Croydon, the unlikely Manhattan of the British insurance world.

The dramatic changes in retailing are obvious enough. Self-service supermarkets with highly computerised price coding and stock control, open-plan banks and building societies, and round-the-clock automatic teller machines. Petrol stations where we service ourselves, and even armchair shopping using viewdata.

It is not the companies that have changed, it is the customer who has revised his or her expectations from suppliers. The view of what is good service has changed dramatically. Good service for most now means minimal human contact and fast service.

If fifteen years ago you had been approached with the following business idea in the catering trade, chances are you would have rejected it without a second's hesitation. The plan is that we open shops selling minced meat patties on untoasted buns. We make people queue up to get served, give them no choice of whether they want the meat well done or rare, no choice of whether they have relish or not (they all do), no choice of whether to put salt and vinegar on the chips. We serve the 'meal' in plastic cartons, do not offer even wooden or plastic knives and forks, and expect people to eat with their fingers. And in order to get the customers out of the shop in as short a time as possible, we will have seats that incline forward so you can't sit on them comfortably for more than a few minutes . . . Oh, and we will also train them to clear their own tables when they have finished.

Despite this, fast food service is now seen as good service, queueing to use an automatic teller in the rain and risking a mugging is now seen as good service and efficient banking, and the architecture and design of shops, garages, offices and even Labour Exchanges – Job Centres – have begun to reflect our new expectations. Increasingly to younger generations, 'good' service really has come to mean minimal service.

We can all regress and regret. Time was when AA men saluted and garages actually put petrol in for you, *and* checked the water and oil. Today, some are even charging for the use of high-tech air-hoses and seem pretty cross if you don't impulse purchase a sack of potatoes, coal and a barbecue set when you pay for your meaningless litres in meaningless new pence. Time was when cheddar cheese tasted like cheese, not soap. I half ate a sandwich recently and discovered they had forgotten to peel the plastic film divider off the cheese slice. It hardly seemed to matter. Time was when only debs 'came out'. Even the talking clock now carries a commercial. And as for telephone boxes – no more button Bs to press, and increasingly just these little foreign-looking canopies with payment only by Phonecards. How things change. An entry appeared in the *Salford City Reporter* about my home town back in 1925. It concerned the first street telephone kiosk, and its last phrase showed remarkable, if unintentional, foresight: 'A public telephone box is to be erected on the pavement opposite 345 Broad Street. This will be the first outdoor telephone box in the town and will, no doubt, be a great public convenience.' How right they were.

Whereas conservatism in dress for individuals still remains sound advice, there are very few businesses for which modernity is now inappropriate in terms of offices – safe modernity that is, with no evidence of conspicuous spending on original Hockneys or Moores.

Does your building and its interior tell your customers, your employees, where you are going? Check it against your positioning statement.

## Corporate Design

Letterheads, logos, business cards, brochures and other literature style and layout, the annual report, the company newspapers, noticeboard paper, the sign outside the factory gate, vans and lorry livery, company uniforms, the layout and design of recruitment ads – all of these things, and others you can think of for your own organisation, are statements about you. Are they up to date, do they communicate the positive messages about the company you want, are they even consistent with each other? Do they fit the positioning statement?

Redesigning a letterhead and logo will not in itself achieve anything very much, but as part of your overall plan to present yourself as you know your customers want to see you, they can be very important.

Once again your positioning statement can form the basis of a brief to a design consultancy to develop a corporate identity. Although not cheap, it is generally better to ask a specialist design firm to develop the work for you. Your normal printer and graphics people could certainly produce some attractive-looking designs, designs you might well prefer at first sight. They are not as likely to be on strategy with your positioning aspirations however, whereas those from a firm used to this specialist type of work should be.

Any corporate design work should aim for authority, style, an immediate 'house' feel appropriate to your business, have the ability to translate easily into other potential media (T-shirts, balloons, banners, memorabilia), and have a long shelf life. I can easily tell a 1960s flowery, trendy corporate identity job, and I have a suspicion that some of the high-tech, computery design of late will look very dated by the early 1990s.

A house colour is also helpful. The safest advice seems to be, if in doubt, go for dark blue.

Remember you should only rethink your corporate identity every ten years or so. Take the time to brief thoroughly and spend the money to get it right. Of all the things you do, altering or totally redesigning your letterhead and business cards will be the most controversial internally. Be prepared for a fight and stick to your guns. After all, the prime role of corporate identity is to reach current and potential outside customers, not to placate irate long-serving salesmen or senior secretaries.

## Corporate Tone and Style

Newspapers and magazines often have style books. They provide a guide *cum dictum* on whether to use an 's' or a 'z' in certain words, on whether Government or government is right, and on general grammatical and style options. Companies should learn from this.

There should be general consistency within the company on spelling options, on writing styles, on the layout of letters and documents, on the tone of voice adopted – literally on the telephone by the operator and secretaries, and figuratively in correspondence, sales brochures and other literature. An officious, curt switchboard operator, a grumpy security guard answering out of hours, a bottom-pinching lift attendant, an over-familiar or garrulous old tea lady can all cause havoc with the best laid positioning plans. So can Victorian-style letters from accounts, careless word-processed standard replies to complaints letters, and amateurish-looking sales literature and trade ads that jar with the confident, forward-looking positioning you will have developed.

Training sessions for anyone interfacing with the public or customers can easily be arranged from national bodies or by local colleges of further education. An office manual can be written giving the rules on layout and style, for newcomers and existing secretarial staff. Senior secretaries should be asked to monitor adherence and conduct spot checks in daybooks. Directors should make a point of ringing in anonymously and sending complaints letters to see the speed and style of response. Award schemes can be launched to motivate people to do better – the Americans are fond of giving people little stars to wear, and the Japanese caps with military-style scrambled egg. In Britain a thank-you from the top, accompanied by a cheque for £50 and a picture in the house journal, is probably more effective.

I once remember hearing Sir Richard Marsh tell the story of how he was leaving British Rail's headquarters late one night in the days when he ran it, and heard a telephone ringing somewhere. He picked it up and an irate passenger demanded to know to whom he was speaking. 'It's Richard Marsh. I'm the chairman,' was the reply. After a pause the man said, 'Good grief, it's come to this. The chairman answering the bloody phone now!'

Bosses should keep in touch, however, and check personally on how customers are dealt with. Most of the big departmental and supermarket chains, for example, expect their directors to make several personal checks a week on their stores, including Saturdays.

So far as practicable, the middle and senior management should know and be able to express the company view on a range of important issues facing the business – be it the end of year results, some international trade negotiations, a change hoped for in the chancellor's budget, relevant health issues, the impact of commodity price and currency fluctuations etc. As soon as the company has a view on such topics, it is helpful if someone writes a summary and distributes it to management in the form of a company briefing note. The osmosis theory of management briefing is very dangerous. The only thing that reliably transmits via osmosis, in my experience, is a bad smell. People should know the company viewpoint and be able to express it consistently to customers, suppliers and employees.

The story of the branch manager on his honeymoon illustrates the point. He climbs into bed on the first night, and immediately falls asleep. His new wife, not at all amused by this, digs him hard in the back and whispers, 'Turn over, darling.'

He replies sleepily, '£10 million in the first quarter.'

A sign of the marriage to come . . .

# PART THREE
## Brand Personalities

# The Brand Personality

## You're Never Alone With A Brand

If companies and organisations can be like people, then this is even more true for products, brands, which can be like familiar old friends.

To American GIs in the war, Coke and Pepsi, Lucky Strikes, Hershie Bars and Wrigley's gum were literally a taste of home, the taste of their girlfriend's last kiss at the quayside.

Some brands really do have a personality, characters real or cartoon, who we have got to know through advertising and packaging. Mr Cube, the Homepride Flour Graders, Mr Kipling, the Bisto Kids, Captain Birdseye, the Milky Bar Kid, Oxo Kate, the Ovaltineys, the Milk Tray Man, the Dulux English sheepdog, Arthur the Kattomeat cat, and of course the PG Tips chimpanzees. Other brands link themselves with existing well known people, mainly from the worlds of show business or sport, whose existing public persona fits well with the way the marketeers want the brand to be viewed.

After the *Endurance* had been lost, crushed in 1912 by ice in the bleak southern seas, Ernest Shackleton, whilst stranded with his crew on an ice flow 346 miles from the nearest food and shelter, salvaged a number of judicious necessities from the fast disintegrating wreck. The first things he subsequently issued were 'a complete new set of Burberrys and underclothing to each man' and 'ten of the Jaeger woollen [sleeping] bags' – surely some small comfort for all with their familiarity from home; truly life-saving placebos.

And however distant from home I am, in India or East Africa, a British Airways sign still makes me feel that home is not after all that far away, and that they would indeed still take more care of me if I needed something. The BBC has the same effect, as do most international hotels – Hiltons, Inter-Continentals – embassies of a kind, all of them, for the lonely disorientated business traveller. We trust great brands.

The Squibb drug company in the US captured a great truth in its first-ever advertising campaign in 1921 – 'The priceless ingredient of every product is the honour and integrity of its maker'. This was just a year before a date on which advertising agency bosses should now bow three times in the direction of their paper millions – 28 August. On that day in 1922, at 17.00 hours, the first-ever advertisement was broadcast, on a New York radio station.

Music can also become part of a brand's personality in advertising, sometimes the leading part. I have mixed views about its use, particularly of snatches of great classical music in this way. Bizet's

March of Carmen has been ruined for me forever by the early Esso sign TV ads – 'the Esso sign means happy mo-tor-ing'; so has Dvorak's New World Symphony by a bread ad; Mahler's 7th by a commercial for motor oil; and Orff's Carmina Burana for aftershave. On the other hand, it could have taken me another ten years or more to discover Delibes' exquisite Lakmé were it not for a stylish British Airways commercial. And I have almost forgiven Frank Muir for singing 'Everyone's a fruit and nut case' to the Dance of the Sugar Plum Fairy from The Nutcracker. Advertising agencies are not totally to blame, however. Ravel's Boléro now has me thinking of panting ice-skaters, or panting thinking of Bo Derek in the film '10'. And Holst's planet suite will be for ever Quatermass.

But please, nobody tell them about Gabriel Fauré or they'll have him in shampoo commercials.

Whereas corporate identity campaigns, when professionally conducted, are relatively low risk activities, any tinkering with an established product brand, be it successful or in decline, can be extremely risky. A brand can have a great many valuable properties, only some of them obvious and measurable. It is all too easy to destroy brand benefits and fail to replace them with anything better, or anything at all. Research helps, but most new products are researched and the majority still fail.

Leading brands even have their own guardians and protectors within the marketing department – brand managers – whose job it is to promote the brand yet remain the steward of its integrity.

Seemingly strange words to use in this connection with a mere product, but real brands are very much more than just a mere product. A Mars Bar, for example, is something we have all grown up with and in the words of the best advertising copy line ever written, in my view, back in 1960, it has helped us work, rest and play. What a marvellous way to present the simple enjoyment of a snack, a chocolate bar. As a consumer, I don't want to see them involved in any kind of nasty promotion, and I don't ever want to see that famous, trusted friend's name and logo cheapened. I don't want that, and you can be sure Mr Mars (yes, there is a Mr Mars) and his marketeers feel just the same way. They won't let me down.

Hoover, Guinness, Fairy Liquid, Singer Sewing Machines, Church's shoes, Persil, Heinz Beans, Parker Pens, Pyrex Ovenware, Rolls Royce Motors, HP Sauce, Christy's towels . . . I trust all of these brands and confidently expect them to behave and perform in certain ways. Some may be in decline for all I know, and their brand managers worried about their modernity, about their relevance to today, and where they fit into their positioning statement to take them to the mid-1990s. But as a consumer, my reaction is extremely conservative. Leave things as they are. Don't tinker with my old friends.

This is the problem often faced, and it is one of the most difficult to tackle. If all the sales and research data really do show a famous brand nose-diving to oblivion within five years, becoming de-listed, over-taken – what to do? Change it and you run the risk of losing what loyal customers and retailers you retain, leave it alone and the final shelf it appears on may be in the Victoria and Albert.

An answer can be to reposition the brand. By conducting very detailed consumer research – quantitative and certainly qualitative – a market opportunity may be found which builds on some of the brand's existing strengths, but takes it into newer areas. As a trial, the repositioned brand, in a new pack design, supported by point of sale and advertising stressing the new niche being targeted, can be test-marketed. This means the familiar product remains on sale in the normal way, except that in one of two TV regions the repositioned brand is sold-in to the retailers and heavily promoted to the customers. The North East, Scotland and East Anglia are often picked for test markets because of their relatively clear geographic and media boundaries. Cheap TV advertising rates are generally available for test market campaigns, and some retail chains have special offers to manufacturers to attract them just to use their stores for the test.

During test marketing, sales are of course carefully monitored, along with consumer and trade reaction. A control region is also designated sometimes in order to gauge as accurately as possible how sales of the repositioned brand are doing compared with existing promotional activity.

The keys to a successful repositioning, or simply to taking an established brand to a new plane, can be many. Audrey Eyton's book *The F-Plan Diet*, for example, gave a whole range of familiar breakfast cereal brands and other food products, like beans, a new lease of life because of their healthy high-fibre content. Keeping up with children's tastes and fads is a constant stimulus to a range of grocery items – cereals like Weetabix, and soft drinks like Kia-Ora, are good examples of long-established brands successfully appealing again to younger audiences. In gardening, the arrival of new technology in the form of hover mowers was the spur to action. The benefits of modern cylinder mowers had been going unnoticed with the introduction of hover machines which, though fun, were inferior to cylinders in virtually every respect. This led to a fierce comparative advertising and PR campaign, which kept cylinder champions Qualcast firmly on top.

An intimate understanding of market needs and of brand personality is clearly fundamental. This can be surprisingly detailed, with in-depth analysis of 'shell values' – that is the obvious proposition(s) of the brand (its unique selling points, its taste, price positioning, visual impact, colour, its role as a badge for peer group status etc) – and the 'yolk values', the properties which contribute almost subliminally to the consumers' perception and enjoyment of the brand (its heritage, its inner strengths, its reassurance values as a kind of placebo etc). Good brand managers can probably tell you more about their brand than about their spouse, and will certainly remember the dates when Nielsen or AGB research data on their sales and market share are due more easily than family anniversaries and birthdays. They can also become great bores as a result of this, seemingly able to talk about nothing but their brand. Talk to the brand manager of 'Chokko-Bar' and try and get him off the subject of his product, market share or his new formulation. Try asking if he's been to the theatre recently as a gambit to talk about something new, and he'll probably say, 'Yes. I was at the theatre last night. Had a marvellous evening. I ate two Chokko-Bars in the interval. And we had great facings on the usherette's tray.'

## Product Packaging

Of course the brand, the product, can remain the same whilst the packaging changes to bring it more up to date, or more into step with what its customers want. As ever, market research will help avoid major mistakes, and mock-ups of the new proposed design on shelves alongside competitors' will show how different and how successful the new treatment will seem to established customers and new. Sometimes design consultancies will recommend a planned introduction of almost imperceptible changes over a period of years, so that customers can hardly tell the difference at any one time, and would be surprised if they saw a ten-year before and after. Many packs have simply had to change in any case to make room for bar-coding, sell-by dates, and required information on ingredients/contents.

The 'pack' can be many things. Many bottles, for example, are highly distinctive and key parts of the brand personality. Heinz Ketchup, Coca Cola, Marmite, Perrier and Bordeaux wine bottles are all instantly recognisable to regular consumers, even if labelling upon them has occasionally changed slightly.

Some companies and organisations use their corporate identity as the overriding brand on each product – such as Heinz with its '57' varieties, Kellogg's and Cadbury with their various breakfast cereal and chocolate products. In these cases there needs to be a degree of across the board corporate identity in terms of packaging, which might limit the ability to do anything too adventurous with just one line which perhaps needs most help. Other companies, such as Unilever, Proctor and Gamble or Rowntree Mackintosh, take a different approach and make little to no use of their corporate identity in individual product branding. Do you know whether Ariel washing power is from Unilever or P&G? Others do a little of both. Mars Bars are clearly from Mars Confectionery, but so are Twix, Maltesers and Marathon – very strong brands in their own rights. These are all key considerations when thinking about alternative pack design.

In-store positioning can be another factor when considering packaging. Where in, say, a supermarket would the customer expect to find you?

As for corporate identity work generally, product packaging is a highly specialised field with only a handful of leading consultancies who attract most of the major jobs. It is far too important to risk getting wrong. As ever, use your positioning statement and commission research as the basis for a thorough brief, involve production and distribution if any cardboard engineering or size changes are being considered, select a consultancy and sweat them until further research and your own intuition as the person closest to the brand produces the results you need. If in doubt, don't change. Developing an established brand calls for vision and bravery, changing it calls for caution and stealth.

## The Role of Brands in Commodity Markets

Brands are principally built and maintained by advertising and advertising considerations, as this superficial look at brand management has made clear. Advertising and distribution remain the main preoccupation. The two are closely linked in any case. Sophisticated retailers expect the brands they stock to be well supported, as well as looking for 'investment' in themselves – on price, on special offers, on joint-store catchment area advertising perhaps. The growth of own label and supermarket brands has mirrored the growth of powerful multiple grocers, similarly mirrored in many other sectors, such as electrical retailing, do-it-yourself, gardening and hardwear.

There is a rising paranoia bubbling under the calmish exterior of many brand management teams today. As retailers become a well-respected brand in their own right (in the way that Marks & Spencer has always been with its St Michael range, for instance); as retailers begin to spot and dictate market trends and sell own-label products themselves (in the way the larger electrical retailers now do); as tea, coffee, biscuits, pet food, flour, bottled water, and so many other items in the family shop become virtual commodities when bought from trusted shops – just what *is* the role of many a brand? This shift in the balance of power between retailers and manufacturers is shown by two stark facts: the top ten per cent of grocery shops now have over seventy-five per cent of sales; and the private label goods of major grocers now account for almost thirty per cent of packaged grocery sales.

Most brands certainly need advertising support, but thanks to media inflation and rising production costs even a million pounds does little to impress these days. And a brand which relies solely on heavy and creative advertising to give it a relevance against good quality own label is surely on very shaky ground. It needs constant support from product innovation, research and development, and from promotions – perhaps label collection schemes or on-pack offers. And it needs to shout regularly and loud to retail buyers and shoppers alike about its real unique selling points – special formulation, quality control, ingredient 'x'

– which top manufacturers should constantly strive to produce. If you talk to top supermarket buyers, their main criticism of manufacturers is the dearth of real product innovation. That is what they now see the real role of manufacturing to be. They themselves can and do source 'commodity' lines direct.

Public relations communications have greater credibility than paid-for advertising – if they come through media relations the reader, viewer or listener knows that the reference to the product or service they pick up has come through the filter of a journalist's pen, working for a publication or programme they like or respect. Staying with the grocery analogy, a favourite magazine describing a new or re-presented vitamin enriched/additive free/low cholesterol/high fibre whatever, will have real benefits to the brand both in its own right and as a way of adding further substantiation to the advertising proposition.

Whatever the product – grocery, industrial, business-to-business, a financial service – initiatives to generate appropriate editorial mention will be an important part of re-enforcing the brand character, and indeed the relevance of the brand in today's consumerist climate. A whole range of brand PR activities can be considered, including:

heavily branded editorial competitions, describing the product and offering it as the prize;

paid-for 'advertorials', where a magazine runs one or more pages featuring your product, normally in specially commissioned photography and on page designs which look like the normal editorial style of the publication;

the carefully managed offer for journalists to try out and review the product or service, comparing it with the opposition or own label if you are sufficiently confident of your uniqueness and quality;

routine 'what's new' product news and updates, so you are featured in round-up columns;

a journalists' factory visit, designed to generate editorial about how you make things and control quality;

a survey, especially commissioned by the brand on the product sector, making you industry spokesman in the media on a topic of consumer interest;

a promotion designed to help to raise money for a charity – perhaps sponsoring some appeal, or a label collection scheme whereby you donate an agreed amount of money for every label sent in;

the preparation of books, booklets, or leaflets giving consumer tips in your sector, which can lead to syndicated feature articles, and the offer to send away with a stamped, addressed envelope;

syndicated feature articles aimed at regional weekly groups, and radio tape interviews on topics of real consumer interest, but with limited branding;

a plan of possible opportunistic news or photocall stories, using periods of high relevant media interest, for example Mother's Day, Christmas, Valentine's Day, the first day of Spring, the Budget, and so on;

the selection and promotion of relevant sponsorships, which should generate publicity and associations sympathetic to your positioning.

These are just some of the types of consumer PR activities which can support a brand. There may well be specialist groups who are highly influential, however, and planned PR activities can be developed to reach them too with your message – people perhaps such as health visitors, home economists, the medical profession, teachers, environmental health officers, trading standards officers, MPs and others. Public relations activities – such as the preparation of special leaflets; attendance at professional and trade exhibitions; seeking to interest trade and professional journals in articles from you; offering yourself as an industry speaker at trade and professional conferences and seminars; inviting selected leaders of the sectors to meet you in a business/semi-business environment and presenting your views to them – all these efforts can hope to achieve is that your views, properly ordered and honestly presented, will be heard by groups important to you. Beyond that, any success in shaking or changing opinions will simply depend on the recipients' opinions of your case. These are healthily cynical groups, people who have been exposed over the years doubtless to some ham-fisted and pretty insulting attempts by special interest groups – people like you – to influence them. On the other hand, they are an interested audience. If you have something new or important to say about your brand or your generic sector, then they need to keep themselves up-to-date.

The group crucially important to any consumer goods manufacturer, however, is the wholesale and retail network. The next chapter looks at the role of research in helping to make the best of your various formal and informal communications with key accounts through to the one-man independents. You really cannot afford to experiment with this group. With competitors snapping at your heels and the constant threat of de-listing haunting you like Banquo's ghost, an off-strategy bright idea to jolly up the trade could have disastrous consequences.

One thing is certain, however. The role of the trade press in keeping your brand and news in front of key people really is important. Virtually every sector will have its trade papers. In the grocery business this includes *The Grocer* and *Supermarketing*. But a moment's thought will demonstrate a wider trade press for important grocery decision-makers. The management of the multiples will read the marketing and advertising trade press, so that becomes important too. Amongst smaller grocery outlets there is now a large and growing number of Asian shopkeepers – in groceries generally, and in confectioners, tobacconists and newsagents (CTNs). They may well read *Asian Trader*, half of which is printed in English, the other half in Gujarati. The finance director, someone with an important influence on your cashflow, will probably read *Accountancy Age*, and the *Financial Times*, a kind of village trade paper in its way. All of them may see an hour-long video of news and views called *Retailing World.*

One trade, the drinks industry, even has a daily trade paper, the *Morning Advertiser.* Travel agents, at the last count, were on the receiving end of no less than six different trade journals each month.

Virtually every trade and profession has at least a couple of trade or professional papers or magazines of direct interest to them, as well as perhaps being attracted by more general business, financial, technical or marketing trade journals. The good news is that the editorial teams all have an awful lot of space to fill and will always be on the look out for genuine news, interesting photographs, and opinionated feature articles from industry figures.

Most trade papers suffer a kind of schizophrenia amongst readers. Familiarity can breed contempt, and most people from time to time dismiss their paper as a 'trade rag'. Certainly some of the pictures used and stories carried sometimes betray a light news week. On the other hand, they are scanned avidly the minute they come in, and the pecking order for who gets a copy to his/herself and who is on, and where on, a circulation list is a good indication of in-company status.

And they always seem full of that bumptious, publicity seeking competitor of yours, don't they? His face grinning at you every week from behind a gin with his fat wife at some trade 'do' or other, or alongside some facile guest feature article you could have written five times better if you'd had time. And why is it that editorial promotions always seem to be with *his* company? He and the publisher seem as thick as thieves. After all, you spend more on trade press advertising than he does. And what's this? He's chief guest speaker now at the rag's annual trade seminar, *and* guest judge for their trainee-of-the-year award scheme. Bloody self-publicist. Just after being head-hunted, that's *his* game . . .

Sounding off to yourself or others like this can be a useful bit of catharsis, but deep down you know you are not doing enough to keep the trade press informed about your brand, not doing enough to assert your brand and yourself as a trade spokesman, one noticed and respected by customers and others. The 'others' are important too. Stockbrokers' analysts, your sponsoring ministry civil servants, MPs who follow your industry and the specialist writers in the national media – including TV – all these people read your 'trade rag'. So, incidentally, does your chairman and MD.

You should have a christian-name relationship with the publisher, editor, and key news and feature journalists and photographers on your trade papers. Swap home numbers; you should develop an internal clock which tells you when their weekly or monthly copy deadlines are approaching, and you should seldom let one pass without a call. Even if you have nothing, just chat, ask what's happening and you may well be invited to comment on some trade story just breaking, of which others will know nothing until they see your quote. Become an off-the-record (not for quoting, for background only) or non-attributable (an industry source said . . .) source of comment and industry figure. You know much more than a busy journalist can about your particular patch; be helpful, consistently accessible and reliable. A real relationship can develop and you will run much less risk of being ignored or misunderstood, and will almost certainly start to irritate that bumptious competitor to boot.

Do severely limit the number of people authorised to comment to trade magazines – and other media – preferably to no more than two. If you work with a public relations consultancy, have them chase and nag you about copy deadlines and forthcoming features; expect them to come to you regularly with planned and opportunist ideas for trade press releases, features and picture stories, but make sure that you or someone you nominate from within the company remains the prime trade press contact for anything other than routine enquiries.

## War Games

You are not doing your job properly as steward of a brand if you are not continuously alert to opportunities and dangers which may arise or can be created by you or your competitors and general trading conditions. Conduct a SWOT analysis. This simply means listing the Strengths, Weaknesses, Opportunities and Threats as you see them, and analyse how they can impact upon your prospects. Double-guessing new marketing and advertising strategies or new product developments from competitors is part of it. Trade gossip will sometimes give clues, a change of advertising agency generally means a new approach. Double-guess it, talk to one of the agencies who failed in the pitch, try and get the brief, decide what your reaction could and should be to the trade, to employees and end customers. Double-guess possible technological breakthroughs or social changes that could help or hinder you – eg the new watch technology, the take-off of compact disc players and their impact on deck manufacturers, the growth of turbo-powered engines and the demands made on the motor oils used, the movement against added salt in foodstuffs, and so on.

What if your biggest competitor suddenly cuts prices and decides to live on lower margins for a couple of years to grab market share from you, or perhaps to use their financial muscle to force you out of the market? What if they increase their pack size for the same price? What if they launch an aggressive 'knocking' comparative advertising campaign directed at your key product?

These are important issues which should be considered in a semi-formal way from time to time, perhaps a couple of times a year at a think tank. You will find the public relations aspects of the 'what if?' game will take up most of your time. Should the stance be calm and above it all, or aggressive and self-confident, mixing-it straight back; should it be the honest-John to the trade, the injured party, the loyal ally of the retailer subject to scurrilous attack?

A brand is a good friend but a hard and ruthless taskmaster. If his steward is not winning his battles and defending him, another knight with shinier armour will be sought. Battles must be anticipated and not just won, but be seen to be won by the trade and the customer. PR can make or break a brand – and any number of brand managers.

## Read This – Get One Free

Sales promotion is an increasingly important part of the brand marketing mix, and the distinction between it and brand public relations is becoming blurred. The best sales promotions have great PR potential anyway. Equally, as creative PR people wrestle with how best to make a brand special, give it a new USP to help sales along at a crucial time, or to protect or increase listings and facings, their minds will often turn to forms of sales promotion.

Often the most affordable sales promotion is to give away extra product for a while – twenty per cent more this month; buy five cans and get one free in a six-pack; collect these vouchers to save for a free can; and so on. Other forms of sales promotion can range from the famous free plastic daffodils and the whisky glasses with petrol purchases, to on-pack offers – send away for this book/cooking utensil/cassette/tracksuit whatever with ten labels and you get it free or cheap. Children love free toys and cut-out characters with packs. Trading stamps were also very popular for a time.

Naturally, you actually have to tell people about your sales promotion, and this can be done through advertising, direct mail or leafleting to customers, and through point-of-sale (POS) material, leaflet dispensers and moving, eye-catching attention-getters on the shelf, known in the heady science of the trade as 'wobblies'. You must also have the permission and support of the retailers, who plan in-store promotions often months ahead. Their staff will need briefing on the promotion, especially if vouchers and tokens are to be redeemed. The larger retailers may well want a 'tailor made', exclusive to them.

For your part you have to talk to designers, to your production, packaging, distribution and sales people about getting things on the label and/or stuffed in. How long will it take to get the new product on the shelf, what's your stock turnaround, how much old stock is out there? Can you get a team of merchandisers round stores to get POS up, make sure the right product is out and improve your impact on the shelf?

Through normal PR channels you can tell the retail trade about the promotion via the trade press – help sell it in – and you can brief your own production, distribution and sales teams through internal channels. If the offer is really novel or if, say, there is a new specially developed book or leaflet that would be of interest to cookery, DIY, gardening, etc, enthusiasts, then media relations can help draw attention to the offer. You might even negotiate from very early on a link with a magazine to tie it in with the retail promotion, or as a separate direct sell offer (introductory only, so as not to cut out the trade) in return for valuable editorial support. Some national newspapers are interested in promotions like this for their own circulation building purposes, and will front page an offer for, say, cans of lager, redeemable from a national off-licence chain if you collect their tokens. If the paper is advertising on TV at the time you will probably be featured on that too.

In fact it was newspapers which gave sales promotion one of the biggest fillips ever in the early 1980s with the 'bingo' war. Started by the tabloid, the *Daily Star*, bingo rapidly swept Fleet Street, with almost every paper needing to respond to the success the *Star* had. Households were sent a bingo card and to win big cash prizes readers had to buy the paper every day to see which numbers had come up. The *Daily Express* set the rest reeling, however, when they brought in the chance for a reader possibly to win a million pounds. No problems there getting TV and radio coverage about that sales promotion. You can go to an insurance underwriter and negotiate a premium to insure yourself against having to pay the million pounds. The size of premium will depend on the odds of it being won of course. It's rather like some golf tournaments who offer a Rolls Royce to anyone getting a hole in one at a certain hole – that can be insured against in the same way.

The very first bingo millionaire in fact came through the *Sun*, with all the attendant free publicity. The *Express* however staged a real cliff-hanger when they had four readers, one of whom was definitely going to win a million, the rest £100,000 each, filmed actually opening the envelopes. This was used later that day as a TV advertisement, again generating considerable publicity.

What the popular Fleet Street bingo eventually proved, however, was that one of the great benefits of sales promotions is their uniqueness at the time to any one brand. They can lead to substantially increased product being sold-in and sold-out, but if everyone starts doing it, as happened, the uniqueness is lost and things cancel themselves out.

Scratchcard/game piece promotions are another popular mechanic for sales promotions, giving everyone the chance to win a big prize, and often giving everyone a little something anyway as a sampler.

All the sales promotions like this need to be checked against the Lotteries Act, or the PR generated can be of a pretty disastrous kind if the promotion has to be withdrawn and prosecution considered.

I am a fan of planned, creative sales promotions – not the panic stations we've got to shift some stock type. Again, as with all other elements of presentation, the brief must be thorough to ensure the campaign is synergistic with the brand's positioning. A good sales promotion is probably the easiest way of all to boost sales and share up towards our twenty per cent target – for a short time at least. If you are brought in to save a brand, turn it around or get high retail stock levels sold out in a short time span, sales promotion is probably your greatest friend.

# Telling Your Story

## Gift or Graft?

List three or four of the most creative people you can think of – Mozart, Monet, Paul McCartney, Graham Greene perhaps.

The temptation is to believe that creativity is some kind of casual gift possessed by classical and contemporary heroes. Mozart was, after all, a child protégé, wasn't he? And Monet, the father of impressionism, what a clever idea *he* had.

The fact is that creativity is eighty per cent training, discipline, hard work and time, and only perhaps twenty per cent natural bent and talent. Child protégé or not, Mozart had total immersion in music through his father virtually from the cradle, and was exposed to a tremendous variety of musical stimuli in his travels very early on in life around Europe. Monet – already famous at the age of fifteen in his home town of Le Havre for his painting – still was forced to work with a well-known disciplined teacher, Gleyre. And both he and Pissarro learned a lot from the study of Turner. McCartney's hard apprenticeship with earlier bands, playing until he dropped in Hamburg, gave him a training and discipline needed for true popular creativity. And don't try telling a master writer like Graham Greene, with over fifty books and plays behind him, that literature is just about creativity and flair.

Good ideas, a quick mind, skill at playing clever games with words – these things are not creativity. And the cliché trappings of creative people – moodiness, flamboyant dress and behaviour, being useless at things *practical* – only present a caricature. Creativity, in fact, is simply a form of problem solving, and so identifying the precise problem to be solved is the first and most important step.

If then eighty per cent of creativity is preparation and hard work, it follows that people who feel themselves weak creatively can make dramatic improvements in their performance by greater application and method. A good creative director of an advertising agency will expect a very full brief before putting his mind to a solution. He or she will want to immerse themselves in the client's industry, its history, in its production processes, quality control procedures, in its corporate style, in the way customers look at the market – all these things and more before outline creative treatments are drawn up. Once the real creative brief has been thoroughly understood, an acceptable creative solution could become obvious to anyone. The skill is in arriving at that very tight brief.

Creativity in invention and new product development is similar. Most great or useful inventions stem from a need identified by people with a direct interest or knowledge in the subject area – be it digital watches or pot noodles. They know what they are looking for before they begin. Wartime is the biggest hothouse for invention, when the need has lives as well as pound notes attached to it.

To improve your own creative performance, stop trying to search for an answer until you have laboriously defined and refined the question. Spend most of your time on thinking of the objectives and the desired results and responses and at least an acceptable piece of workmanlike 'creativity' will follow – perhaps even better. And give yourself time. One of the greatest failings in so-called uncreative people is this erroneous belief that all that is needed is a bright idea from someone – and that can only take a few minutes. Free-ranging creative brainstormings tend to follow from this and are, on the whole, a bad idea. They are almost always poorly briefed, and people just throw around sparky ideas to show off – whether on strategy or not. If creativity is a form of problem solving, it follows that the ability to implement and follow through proposed solutions must be resolved. Accept that creativity is long, hard work and you will have got over the biggest hurdle.

One of the best ways of improving your creativity is through the use of Synectics. W. J. J. Gordon published a book of that name in 1961, and the leading exponents of Synectics are Synectics Inc of Cambridge, Massachusetts, and Synectics Ltd in Leighton Buzzard in the UK, who run training courses. Synectics is in effect a methodology, developed from over twenty-five years of research and experience, designed to encourage effective innovation. It has proved that the techniques, skills and strategies required to encourage 'creativity' can be taught and learned.

## Public Relations and Creativity

It is safer to aim for being a bit different, not a whole lot different. Dare to be a Daniel, to stand out, but within limits prudent to your business. Richard Branson's audacious Virgin Atlantic Challenge to bid for the Blue Ribband Cup was very appropriate to his record-buying and airline-passenger target market on both sides of the Atlantic, and for a stylish, exciting, young and thrusting company. It would have seemed wrong for British Airways as an established airline, or for Woolworth or Boots, two of the largest record retailers in the country. But for Virgin it achieved for two consecutive years the kind of exciting and well-positioned media coverage that leaves other PR professionals for once speechless with admiration.

PR creativity again is all about hard thinking and planning. Opportunist things can and do come along, but most 'opportunism' can be planned. It can be as 'creative' as checking for anniversaries – of, say, a key account's fiftieth year, or the trade paper's tenth, and six months before planning a big or small initiative of some kind. Perhaps with the major multiple you could run a special promotion in-store, investing in them, offering customers some benefit to celebrate fifty years of their favourite store courtesy of you, one of their longest suppliers.

For the trade paper, you could throw a special party for the editorial and advertising teams (all important to you) with a cake, candles, the whole lot. You might run a celebratory advertisement. You might suggest a joint editorial promotion with prizes from you and branding for you, looking back over ten years' highlights in the trade (well featuring your own brand). Your competitors would be cross at themselves for not thinking of this first, for not being as creative as you. But things like this, which can be very beneficial in terms of trade relationships, are not really creative. They merely show somebody has thought ahead.

Valentine's Day, Mother's Day and the rest, as already mentioned, can give other pegs for 'routine' but seemingly creative ideas.

New product launches and sales conferences call for creativity. Again the best creative ideas are borne out of disciplined thinking well in advance. When launching a new rotary lawnmower range featuring safe plastic cutters rather than the traditional metal blades, Qualcast conducted dramatic demonstrations in hotel rooms and on lawns to gardening journalists. They ran over a shoe with a typical metal-bladed hover mower, which has blade tip speeds of 200mph. It was sliced open, showing just what would have happened to someone's foot in an accident. They also ran the metal-bladed hover over a length of electrical lead, showing how easy it is to float over your mower cable, with the lethal dangers that has. Then they conducted the same tests with the new Qualcast Orbital safety mowers, demonstrating that they did not even nick the shoe or cable. This, allied to official statistics presented on the number of mowing accidents a year, perfectly positioned the new machines.

Back to Virgin Atlantic. When they launched the new airline, Richard Branson came into the press conference wearing a Biggles-style flying helmet and goggles. Had I been asked as someone who knows the airline and travel industry well, I would have strongly counselled against this, arguing that airlines are a serious business and people want reassuring that they will be safe and in the hands of responsible people – the conventional wisdom. I would have been wrong. What Branson and his team realised was that people now know they can take airline safety for granted, in the same way they no longer need to worry about banks or building societies going bust with their savings. What Virgin Atlantic was offering – its points of difference – was great value and fun, so that was what the press conference also communicated. As for Virgin's inaugural flight, those lucky enough to have been on it still talk about it with a kind of hazy, self-satisfied smirk on their face.

When British Airways not long afterwards launched their new livery to important customers and the media, they did it at Heathrow with one of the most spectacular laser shows ever staged, revealing a Boeing 737 in its new Sunday best. The show cost hundreds of thousands of pounds – as did a spectacular light and firework show on the Thames to celebrate their flotation on the stock market. That was as right for British Airways as a Biggles flying-hat was for Virgin's boss.

Whatever the new product, it can only be launched as a *new* product once, and given the normal long lead times for product innovation there can be no excuse for rushed, ill-thought out launches. Creativity is not just something to work for in the consumer goods industries of course. A new generation of water-jet looms, of industrial lubricants, a new government scheme for the unemployed, for small businesses, a new charity, a new banking service perhaps for the self-employed, a new generation of main frames – whatever the product and service, *appropriate* creativity, developed from a clear commercial objective and planned well in advance, will be needed.

Sales conferences can be the annual creative nightmare for the marketing and sales teams, as well as the MD who may well be expected to give yet another Gettysburg address. Some sales conferences are purely designed to brief, motivate and perhaps train the sales force, others are rather designed to present the brand and where it's going to customers, some do both using virtually the same presentation, despite the very different objectives for each audience.

There have been sales conferences held in Iceland to watch the aurora, on Concorde and on cruise liners in the Caribbean. TV, sports and film stars have been used to front them. Highly sophisticated multi-screen audio visuals, live video and laser shows have been used. Quiz show, jury-room and space-ship sets have been created. The evening's entertainments have included top recording stars, comedians, dance orchestras, dance troupes, firework displays, military bands to girls coming out of cakes, and cakes coming out of girls I shouldn't wonder.

The annual pursuit for somewhere new and some way new to present things has in some organisations become seemingly more important than whether a sales conference needs holding at all, and if so precisely what its objectives are. Sales teams have a tough job and an annual perk may be necessary, but it should not be the sales conference. Equally, companies should not feel the need to spend the amount of executive time as well as money that some do simply to win the attention of their own people. If you raised and refurbished the *Titanic* and flew them to it in a flying saucer, salesmen would still complain and want something better next year. Customers in turn might just be forgiven for rethinking their margins given all this conspicuous expenditure. Don't compete with yourself, or the annual sales conference, along with the choice of company Christmas card, will become virtually a full-time job for someone.

The content of any sales or other company conferences is the important thing. Your audience spends most of its waking hours involved in the business, so never underestimate the natural interest they will have in real company or brand news, the latest advertising strategy, research findings, competitor analysis, whatever. You must, again, think well ahead what it is you want your audience both to absorb and do as a result of your efforts. Nothing too complicated and not too much at any one time. Breakaway syndicate sessions are becoming popular for delegates to really get to grips with a new line or strategy, making it interactive, which because of size or conference packaging, most events are not.

The MD's role at these events is important in that it clearly links his or her authority and commitment to the sales and marketing strategy. If there are hard decisions to be faced the MD should be seen to be involved with them. If the theme of the conference is the 'management of change' or the 'need for change' (which with 'towards the year 2000' must take the award for cliché of the millennium)) and the general proposition is that change is necessary, people will comfortably nod in agreement and switch off. If on the other hand the MD says 'There are going to be changes,' then everyone's attention is guaranteed, without the need for a single laser show or piece of Van Gellis electronic AV music. Perhaps that's as 'creative' as you need to be. Direct and businesslike.

## Creative Writing

Writing falls into much the same category as creativity. Some people hate writing, dread it and are convinced that they can never improve. Again, eighty per cent of good writing is preparation, really understanding the objectives of the task, and the hard work of getting it down and drafting and re-drafting. As for creativity, most 'poor writers' are convinced that good writing is a gift from birth and that's that. They also fail to give themselves enough time, believing they need deadlines to write to, like some green eye-shaded hack reporter in a thirties movie. A common, derogatory nickname for bad writers in companies is 'Scoop Higgins', or whoever. The opposite is the truth of course. Deadlines are the last thing a poor writer needs to reach competence.

For those with a problem of spelling or vocabulary, then a dictionary and *Roget's Thesaurus* will rescue you.

I have only three additional general tips. The first is that few things suffer from being twenty per cent shorter, and that goes for the length of words used as well as the length of sentences, paragraphs and the piece overall. You will find it takes longer to write a short speech or article than a long one. The second is, before you start, to compose an eight-word *Daily Express*-style headline which sums up the most vital message you want the reader to remember. You will not use that headline, but once you have finished writing, read it over and see if you really think that message jumps out sufficiently strongly. If not, you know what to do.

Thirdly, borrow from the storyteller's craft and give your piece a beginning, a middle and an end. The beginning should attract, surprise and perhaps challenge the reader to win attention, the middle should develop your argument, and the end recall the main message or surprise which you want to leave with your reader – perhaps picking up again on a theme from your catchy introduction.

There follows a short story of mine which was first published in the *Sunday Telegraph Magazine.* I include it not as some kind of role model (read Capote, Somerset Maugham or Maupassant for that), but simply as the best way I know to illustrate how much can be said in a short piece. It is less than 700 words long. If whole worlds, places and characters can be created and stories told around them using just a few hundred words, surely we can all convey most pieces of business information no less succinctly.

## The Headhunters

Henry was excited as he straightened his tie in the bedroom mirror. 'Sharp at ten,' the headhunters had said, and he was determined not to be late. The interview could well be the turning point in his career. Certainly he had long ago come to the decision that he would go no further with his current employers. The Head Accountant was still in his early fifties; and there could be no promotion other than in dead men's shoes in the small engineering firm's accounts department.

That was why Henry had been so thrilled by the unexpected call a few days earlier. It was from J. Paul and Co Ltd, a new firm of executive search and headhunters as they described themselves. Was he happy with his current prospects as *Assistant* Head Accountant? No? Well they had an international client looking for a new Head, and they were offering a car, a guaranteed income of £18,000 for the first year and a ten per cent share of profit from sales revenue directly attributable to his personal contribution. Was he interested in talking?

Naturally Henry had agreed to be discreet about the proposition until all the loose ends had been tied up. He had even agreed to their suggestion not to tell Muriel, his wife. This was not an unusual request from the clients of headhunting firms. They know that the hardest thing on earth is to keep executive searches secret. He had simply told the secretary he shared with the Head Accountant that he would be at the dentist that morning and not to expect him until 11.30am at the earliest.

Muriel commented on his smartness as he went down for breakfast.

'That's your wedding shirt,' she said. 'Got something special on today?' They had been married less than a year.

'Having lunch with the auditors,' he lied.

'I'll just make up a salad for dinner tonight then if you're having a large lunch.'

'Fine, darling.' He was too excited to think about food anyway: £18,000, a car and a share in profits. Not bad for a twenty-six-year-old. How marvellous it would be if he got the job. He would take her out to dinner and tell her that way. It would make such a difference, the extra money. And they could sell the old Austin Mini.

At 9.55am Henry was pressing the bell at the Victorian office block. There was no sign saying J. Paul & Co, but he was sure it was the right address.

A porter showed him up to the first floor, knocked gently on the door and left him without speaking. Henry was sweating and he nervously flattened his hair as he waited, wishing he'd had a haircut.

The smooth-looking man who opened the door and ushered him to a chair looked about forty – he was a foreigner, Asian maybe, or perhaps from the Pacific.

'Let's have a drink first,' he smiled genially.

Henry tasted the poison in the coffee, but it made no difference. He was dead within half a minute and laid out ready in the white-tiled cellar in five.

The gleaming new Ford was driven up to Henry's house an hour later. Muriel noticed it when she returned from shopping. When she was inside the house she picked up the envelope. Inside she was surprised to find the car keys and a banker's draft for £18,000 from a numbered Swiss bank account. She was even more surprised when Henry did not come home that night, and devastated when, after a week, the police began to hint gently that they were not optimistic about finding him.

The final link with the mystery came a month later, when the Borneo businessman from J. Paul & Co Ltd anonymously sent her a further banker's draft for £7,200, ten per cent of the net profit made on the sale of the shrunken head. White men's heads fetch the highest prices from collectors in the Middle East and Africa. Henry's fetched a record £100,000.

Report, letter, press release and speech writing is not the same as short story writing – the objectives are very different, one primarily to convey information the other primarily to entertain – but I think the differences can be over-emphasised at the expense of the similarities. To win and retain attention with spoken English, we generally accept the need for an element of entertainment. A certain amount of style and panache, entertainment, can even find its way into business-report writing.

Some of the most effective writing in terms of short, sharp communication can be found on those post cards in newsagents windows in red-light areas. You know the kind of thing: 'Young, nubile model. Busty, blonde and well disciplined'. I'm making a serious point. The economy of those eight words and their unambiguous message could give even the best copywriters a run at the next advertising industry awards. So could the girl's media buying.

## Speechwriting and Speechmaking

I spent almost three years as the speechwriter for the director-generals and presidents of the Confederation of British Industry, and I can honestly say that the worst speech I have ever had to sit through was one I wrote myself. It went down well enough on the day and the tycoon who delivered it seemed happy, but its reasonable reception had much more to do with the stature of the man and his office than it did with my over-long, over-ambitious speech.

At the time I was writing an average of three to five speeches *a week* on different topics for different people, at least one or two of which were going to be press-released and possibly recorded for radio and TV.

Most people speak at around 130 words a minute, and they like to ad lib a little, especially at the beginning and the end. I used to estimate a 2,500 word speech to be about twenty minutes, 2,000 about fifteen. Interestingly, when you write for different people you find yourself having to adopt quite different styles to suit the nature of the people. Of course, all important people write some of their own speeches themselves and parts of others, and none would ever read out something a speechwriter had drafted if he or she did not agree with the content or feel comfortable with the style. On the other hand, beware of the people who say I *always* write my own speeches. *Really* important people are far too busy for that – ask any prime minister or president.

It is a presidential speech which is commonly acknowledged to be perhaps the greatest speech in relatively recent history, in terms of literary style and content. In the UK it is a bit like the Domesday Book – everyone has heard of it but few have read it. Unlike the Domesday Book, however, it is very short – just 267 words.

The Gettysburg address was delivered in November 1863 by President Abraham Lincoln at the dedication of a cemetery at the Gettysburg battlefield, and it recalled the great principles of equality established by America's founding fathers.

> *Fourscore and seven years ago our fathers brought forth on this continent a new nation, conceived in liberty and dedicated to the proposition that all men are created equal.*
>
> *Now we are engaged in a great civil war, testing whether that nation, or any nation so conceived and so dedicated, can long endure. We are met on a great battlefield of the war. We have come to dedicate a portion of that field as a final resting-place of those who here gave their lives so that the nation might*

*live. It is altogether fitting and proper that we should do this.*

*But, in a larger sense, we cannot dedicate – we cannot consecrate – we cannot hallow – this ground. The brave men, living and dead, who struggled here, have consecrated it far above our poor power to add or detract. The world will little note, nor long remember, what we say here, but it can never forget what they did here. It is for us the living, rather, to be dedicated here to the unfinished work which they who fought here have thus far so nobly advanced. It is rather for us to be here dedicated to the great task remaining before us – that from these honoured dead we take increased devotion to that cause for which they gave the last full measure of devotion; that we here highly resolve that these dead shall not have died in vain; that this nation, under God, shall have a new birth of freedom, and that government of the people, by the people, for the people, shall not perish from the earth.*

A speech to a trade association or sales conference may seem pretty far removed from the Gettysburg address – but again the similarities are stronger than the obvious differences. Brevity, knowing your audience, having a message and delivering it with style, memorably, should be features shared by all speeches and speakers.

Remember the beginning, middle and end requirement. Remember your need to fine tune the objectives of the speech – and of the organisers in asking you. Remember that most speeches can be shortened to good effect. One story goes of someone making an interminable speech when, after forty minutes, he said: 'I haven't got my watch with me: I hope I'm not going on too long.' A voice from the back shouted: 'There's a calendar behind you!'

Another is of a famous British ambassador to Washington who, fishing for compliments from his wife when returning from a speaking engagement, asked how he had done. Wearily she replied that his speech, as ever, had put him in the Rolls Royce class. He preened himself still further and asked what she meant. 'You were well-oiled. Inaudible. And looked as though you could go on for ever,' came the frosty reply.

Time yourself, and make allowances for the fact that you will probably talk a little faster on the day. Also practise your method of delivery. Don't wave your arms about or modulate your voice like some bad Victorian actor playing melodrama – but do use visual and voice emphasis to introduce pace and variation. Otherwise you drone and bore.

Humour should be left to the experienced speaker, unless you have one or two (no more) very safe in-jokes for your audience, best when directed at yourself.

Many people recommend inexperienced speakers to use cards to fit into the palm of your hand containing just headings to prompt you. Don't ever *read* a speech they warn. I disagree with this, and even though I am now an experienced public speaker, I still quite often use fully written-out speeches. In practice I do use them as prompts, but see nothing wrong in reading either, so long as you keep good eye contact with the audience. For inexperienced speakers I certainly recommend it, for its placebo effect alone. Any questions and answers, of course, are off the cuff, but rehearsed and anticipated.

With good preparation and rehearsal, and a bit of luck, you should never really fail. After all, they have asked you or your organisation to speak in the first place. The luck is always important, however. Remember President Kennedy's famous speech *'Ich bin ein Berliner'*? Imagine if he'd had to give it in Frankfurt, or Hamburg . . .

# Research and Destroy?

Knowing what your audience – your customers and others – *really* want from you, should be line one of any corporate business plan.

Research can destroy deeply held preconceptions about a company or its products, and as it is independent and reasonably scientific, it can help achieve acceptance of often unpalatable truths. It can tell us what others think of us, and equally important it can reveal what important groups like customers want from suppliers and providers of goods and services like ourselves. Sometimes research will confirm your intuition, sometimes it will confound you, sometimes it will shade your views.

That 'profit' was a dirty word with workers was a common belief amongst senior businessmen, many of whom had unshakeable views on the need to drop the word for something less emotive in their company reports and employee newspapers. The word 'surplus' was a front runner.

In my time at the Confederation of British Industry in the late 1970s we commissioned research company MORI to find out what employees really believed. In fact only eight per cent thought that profit was a dirty word. Ninety-eight per cent agreed that companies need profits to plough back into the company and eighty-nine per cent thought it fair to pay dividends to shareholders.

What we learned from the research was that there was nothing wrong with the word profit, and that employees fully understood the need for company profits. They did however have disturbing gaps in their understanding of the *level* of profits needed, thinking that profits were generally too high. After all, a million pound profit for even a large company sounds like an awful lot of money to most people, especially if management never takes the trouble to relate profits to turnover and capital employed. If you are not familiar with big figures they can easily confuse. For example, the earth is either 93,000,000 miles away from the sun or 142,000,000 miles. Do you know which? If not any keen schoolboy astronomer would think you an illiterate fool. (In fact, the earth is 93 million and Mars 142 million miles away from the sun respectively.)

A great deal of time and money is wasted on communications directed at the wrong targets, feeding the wrong messages and attempting to dispel the wrong myths. Time to research and destroy.

Much has been said so far about communication – presenting and projecting facts and images about corporations, products and people.

Research is also a process of communication, but is instead at the listening end of the process. It is about hearing what people have to say, not being heard. This is possibly why some natural communicators find it a little difficult to accept the role of research. When all their experience has led them to inform people, to sell to them, they are not always inclined to stop and listen to what might be being said back.

No communications policy will work satisfactorily, however, if the need to listen is ignored. That 'bridge to engine room' style of management may have sunk the *Bismark*, but it has no place in the modern industrial and commercial world.

There are four key research stages in developing a structured plan of communication:

- *finding out where we and our competitors are now*
- *exploring where we might want to be*
- *exploring how to get there*
- *establishing progress, and in effect asking the first question again, where are we now?*

This type of research plan can also be an invaluable measurement and evaluation of the effectiveness and worth of the communications plan, be it advertising, direct mail, PR or various combinations.

Later we shall look at the methodology of researching these questions, but first to analyse each stage further:

*Where we are*
This in turn breaks down into a number of further questions:

*Awareness – who has heard of my company/product?*
*Familiarity – how well do they feel they know it?*
*Usership – who uses/buys it?*
*Usage – how do they use it?*
*Perception – what is it known for, and what are its strengths and weaknesses?*
*Feeling – what do people feel about my company/product?*

Research into these questions will give a detailed insight into who your customers are and why and how they use your organisation's products or services. Comparative questioning for major competitors will often be undertaken to position the company in its market place.

Be warned, this stage of research can prove pretty traumatic. Your awareness, when unprompted by the researchers, is unlikely to be as high as you believed even on your worst scenario, and your vulnerability in the market place may be starkly exposed. Many an advertising budget has grown out of the alarm which research at this point can create.

*Where we might be*
Having established where you are, it is time to form a view as to where you might be. The time span for this question is also important. Japanese companies in particular take extremely long views of where they are going in ten years time and more.

Account must be taken of the competition, their position and aspirations. Sometimes the competition can be defined too narrowly. A brand of tea is not only competing with other brands of tea, but with any drink, refreshment or pick-me-up the customer may choose. Consumer durables like washing machines are in essence competing for a share of net disposable income against any number of other products and services, from a package holiday to double-glazing.

*How to get there*
An ever more precise strategy is now becoming possible to take us where we want to be.

It is at this point that we must identify and select our key benefits or points of difference, something that will credibly draw our customers, shareholders, employees or whoever, towards appreciating our unique strengths as a company or product. This is possibly the single most vital thing to identify in any communications strategy – the benefit, as it relates to our key audiences.

Robin Wight, chairman of leading international communications company, the WCRS Group, describes this as the process of interrogating a product until it confesses its strengths.

The benefit may be some specific product or performance point of difference – washes whitest, tastes better, lasts longest, etc – or it can be emotionally based: for caring mums, 'the right one', and so on.

To support the benefit there will be a need for evidence, stories, images and a tone and style that communicates what we need. Research will show whether the communications being put out – advertising, PR, pack design – are delivering the message intended, and if so how forcefully.

Managers spend most of their waking hours thinking about their industry and their product and it comes as a nasty surprise when research reminds us that most people don't give a damn about our brand or our market most of the time. Typically, consumers are much more preoccupied with relationships, family, their own job, their home, health, food, drink, friends, and perhaps a special interest like football or gardening.

Learning this is good for us. It helps us put things into perspective and realise how difficult it is to influence those precious few moments when the consumer or broker's analyst actually *is* having to think about us – the shopper's hand hovering in the shop between two branded tins of beans and an own label; calculator in the broker's hand, and judgement waivering between a sell or hold recommendation to investors. It is during these crucial one or two seconds that we find out if all our communications are working as well as we hope, when the emotional and irrational factors come into play, when quite simply you become a winner or loser.

There is a paradox here. On the one hand we can argue that people's reactions to most things in the commercial field – and certainly to products and brands – are fairly incidental, superficial and instant. On the other hand we can see that responses to, say, brand choice, can touch on deep emotional issues and needs. It is here that the brand personality or the company can hold sway. People sort brands and corporations much as they sort people, relating the first impressions to previous experience – good or bad. We take superficial signals and impressions and sort them for convenience into a series of pigeon-holes. Once formed, these perceptions are notoriously difficult to shift, because it is not convenient to do so. It entails a change of mind and as there is no absolute truth in such matters, it is easy to defend and post-rationalise a first opinion for reasons of self-esteem.

The triggers for this categorisation are many – colour, design, name, smell, texture, the ambience in which it is first experienced. The way the mind works may give further clues. Transactional analysis explores man's drives and Canadian psychiatrist, Dr Eric Berne, suggests to us three ego states: Parent – the stage when values, beliefs and prejudices are becoming lodged, influenced by both the maternal, the caring, nurturing parent, and the critical disciplinary paternal parent; Adult – the rational state drawing on observable facts; and Child – the emotional stages, calling upon feelings and intuition. Whatever the many and varied behavioural triggers, it is clear that your little company or brand has quite a task to face in winning acceptance.

At best, companies and brands can achieve a sense of 'belonging' to their consumers, becoming badges or symbols of some aspect of our lives. The newspaper we choose to be seen reading is perhaps the best example of this. It is a statement about oneself, more conscious than most. Car marques are similar. Not just the BMWs and Jaguars, but other less expensive cars such as the east European Ladas which perhaps denote robustness, no frills, and value for money; and then there is the man or woman who always drives a small Ford or Volkswagen, or a Citroen Deux Cheveux. The supermarket we shop at is another badge, worn consciously, along with our perfumes and aftershaves, logos on our clothes, and, perhaps, our wristwatch. A man ordering a pint of draft Guinness is making a statement about himself – and even more so the woman who also orders a glass. Much cigarette branding is based heavily on lifestyle badging, and advertising/ sponsorship-led product identity, although to non-smokers like me any cigarette is a badge for all kinds of negative associations.

Single-minded, carefully targeted communications can help rational-ise and, as often as not, post-rationalise our decisions. Public relations techniques can generate and sustain these badges and flush out many of the things to which the blunt instrument of advertising can only allude – providing more examples, more sensations to project and re-enforce impressions.

The need for research in this psychological minefield is self-evident, research to help us understand companies and products from these many perspectives, from the fairly superficial to the more in-depth, from the picture now to the picture as it might be.

This provides a convenient way of classifying the types of research to help in this process: descriptive research, and exploratory or prescriptive research.

## Descriptive Research

Normally, though not exclusively, descriptive research will use quantitative techniques. These can range from –

**Audits and panels:** these produce market sizes, brand shares, buyer profiles etc, and are the marketing brand manager's most important guide to the product's performance on the shelf. Nielsen and AGB are the best known examples. You have to subscribe to receive these services.

**Omnibus surveys:** regular national studies are carried out on a representative sample of the population or study-group and you can buy into them on an ad hoc basis. Straightforward awareness, usage and 'simple response' questions can be placed. This is a relatively inexpensive way to obtain a large sample view of you, your product or of some issue affecting you. NOP, RSGB, Marplan, Gallup, MORI and MAS are some of the leading organisations offering this service.

**Large ad hoc studies:** more expensive, these can cover usage and attitude behaviour in greater depth.

**Street surveys:** everyman's idea of what market research is – someone with a clipboard stopping you in the street. Although abused of late by some organisations selling financial services, street surveys, when properly conducted by people authorised by the Market Research Society, remain a quick and cheap way of measuring awareness and instant response. Most research companies can organise street surveys on an ad hoc basis.

**Telephone surveys:** another form of speedy research, although they can be used to some extent for qualitative, exploratory questions too. The main problem tends to be the absence of any visual stimulus. This form of research is especially useful for targeting busy audiences, such as businessmen, supermarket buyers, and journalists. Many companies offer telephone research facilities – Audience Selection and Telephone Research being two of the most prominent.

**Hall tests:** these straddle the descriptive and exploratory/prescriptive barrier. They entail literally bringing passers-by into halls to look at or experience products, pack designs or advertisements. They are especially useful where visual stimuli are needed. Most research companies can arrange hall tests, in whatever parts of the country are required.

## Exploratory or Prescriptive Research

**Group discussions:** these are used to explore motivation, perception and attitudes in great depth. The sessions can last one to ten hours, or even longer with a small group of between four and ten. A wide range of qualitative research companies and consultants will arrange and lead group discussions. Frequently a tape recording is made of the discussions, with the participants' consent, so that the often anonymous client can listen to it later.

**In-depth discussions:** these are extended interviews with individuals, often very important opinion leaders, people not likely to agree to attend a group discussion. Again a wide range of firms will conduct in-depth discussions.

**Extended group sessions:** if it is necessary to explore a company, market and brand in even greater depth, this may mean convening a session for long periods of three hours or more. Projective and interactive techniques such as role-playing can be employed.

**Psychographics:** amongst the various ways in which researchers attempt to analyse markets and identify consumers within them is psychographics. This is based on the assumption that people can be defined by more than just their occupation, income, or even where they live (as in the ACORN analysis approach) – that purchasing or other forms of behaviour can be explained or predicted by the way people think or feel, or by their lifestyle and their attitudes to it. In other words, even people in the same class will vary enormously in their attitudes.

Various psychographic systems have been developed – for example, VALS: Value and Life Style, operated by Taylor Nelson & Associates in the UK – although most research companies will conduct psychographic research if requested. The VALS approach is very broad-based and has led to such terms as 'inner-directed' and 'outer-directed', 'self-fulfillers' and 'belongers'.

Other classifications may group housewives, for example, as 'extravagant shoppers' vs 'bargain hunters'; self-confident, sophisticated or health-conscious shoppers vs what some call the 'Coronation Street' housewife.

Even the recent trend to categorise people such as 'Sloanes', 'Yuppies' or 'Young Fogies' is a form of psychographics, describing not just a life-stage, but an approach to life, to acquiring products and using services such as Filofax, BMW Cabriolets, green wellingtons etc.

Experienced researchers understand the role such measurement can play in marketing, and they can use or evolve systems as relevant as possible to the areas they want to study.

This brief canter through the world of formal research demonstrates why large firms, especially those in fast-moving consumer goods (FMCG), employ research managers. Selecting the right research company for your needs can be an art in itself. As a starter, the Market Research Society, 175 Oxford Street, London W1R 1TA produces a yearbook containing the names of most research companies in the UK.

As in programming computers, however, the Garbage In – Garbage Out theory applies. A piece of research can only be as valuable as the brief, and this comes with experience.

As good a way as any to begin to understand yourself and your research needs is to conduct some crude research of your own. Conduct a communications audit on your company or on your brand. As before, the end benefit is likely to be in what it tells you about yourself, and the gaps in your knowledge of your own communications chain.

**Read on for the DIY Communications Audits**

Make a haphazard list of all the people with whom your company communicates. It will be a long list, and will include all or most of the following:

- customers
- suppliers
- employees
- trade unions
- shareholders/the City
- the local community
- bankers
- the taxman
- your trade association
- 'the media'
- local government
- MPs/MEPs/peers
- civil servants
- industry analysts

These are the target audiences for your various communications.

Next prioritise the list into, say, the top three target audiences. Unless you have some pressing environmental or political problem these are likely to include:

- customers
- shareholders/the City
- employees

It soon becomes clear that these broad headings are not adequate. Analyse each further:

**Customers:** for many businesses customers will broadly categorise into key· accounts/the major national and regional multiples, and the independents. They may be further broken down by sales territories, by credit and non-credit customers. Also for the key accounts there may be a pecking order within each customer — the day to day buyer you deal with, his buying director, and his senior general management. Each will need a different style and frequency of communication from you. Then there are existing customers, lapsed customers, and customers from whom you would like to get a listing; there are domestic customers, export customers and agents.

List how you currently communicate with your various customer audiences:

- sales calls
- key account meetings
- sales conference for buyers
- trade and consumer advertising
- mailers/catalogues/price up-dates
- presentations to customer's own sales conferences
- through the trade press and national media
- through trade associations, industry seminars and conferences
- trade shows and exhibitions
- through planned hospitality etc.

Estimate how much all this communication costs you in terms of management time, print and production, conference and exhibition stand costs, and the rest. Then put yourself in the shoes of a key buyer and rank the various methods of communication in order of influence and importance. If he were asked by one of our research people what form of supplier communication he finds most important, what would he say? And what tone and style work best? Is it the big-production-number pushy sales conference, is it the trade show stand you agonise over, or is it a couple of businesslike meetings to talk turkey followed by some phone calls?

**Shareholders/the City:** this target audience may include institutional shareholders, smaller private shareholders, the banks, stockbrokers and other City analysts, the Stock Exchange, divisions, employees and, of course, the City press.

List how you currently communicate with these important audiences:

- full year and interim results, annual report and AGM, employees' report
- chairman's briefings
- periodic presentations to fund managers and bankers
- on and off the record briefings on the company and the sector for brokers' analysts.
- through City press comment
- trade, consumer or any corporate/City advertising

Ask how well this is all working and how prepared you would be, for example, to defend a hostile bid. If you are publicly owned, when did you last inspect your register of shareholders? Have you monitored it for any significant changes? What percentage of the shares are in the hands of institutions? As for the private shareholders, have you analysed how long each shareholder has held them – a reasonable yardstick of likely loyalty. Why not start a procedure whereby the chairman automatically sends a personalised word-processed letter to all new shareholders welcoming them and thanking them for their confidence in your company. As for the more influential City press (the *FT*'s Lex column remains far and away the most important), do you have a record of their last personal contact with your company, and what their own cuttings files are likely to throw up if they had to produce a story to a deadline about, say, an unexpected bid for you?

**Employees:** again there are many different sub-groups requiring different types of communication: the board (executive and non-executive directors), production, line and supervisory management, shop-floor workers, administrative and distribution staff, finance, personnel, sales and marketing etc, head office if you are a division.

List how you currently communicate with these various groups:

- team briefings
- works councils
- the noticeboard
- the house journal
- company conferences
- video
- trade and national advertising

- employees' and shareholders' annual reports
- the trade and national press
- through trade union channels etc

Again estimate how much all of this costs, and which means of communication work best. If different groups were grilled by a researcher, what would they list as the most important sources of information about the company, its products and its progress? The canteen grapevine or the house journal, their supervisors or their shop stewards?

You will have discovered that you are almost certainly unsure of how you really are communicating in practice to these three groups of important target audiences, and that rather like advertising, you think you're wasting half your communication budget, but don't know which half.

The solution may now be to commission professional research to help you find out, or be more disciplined in the briefing and monitoring of what you are currently doing.

Whatever, another important step has been taken towards raising the performance of your communications activities. You will have a much clearer idea of what is wanted and expected of you, and how better to manage the flow of communications to deliver all of this. We look next in even more depth at one of the target groups, by conducting an employee communications audit.

Whether you commission an outside consultancy to conduct or counsel you on an employee communications audit, or do-it-yourself, what you will be looking for at the end of the process are facts, not opinions. Experience shows that managers are much more likely to take action and decisions as a result of objective evidence rather than someone's interpretation of a set of employees' opinions. Inevitably though when you collect facts you cannot help gathering opinions as well, although the reverse is not always true.

A successful audit will show how effective an organisation is in communicating with and involving its employees. It will find out how the organisation is actually doing rather than what it thinks it is doing in terms of effective communication. The hallmarks of a good audit are that it is:

- short
- objective
- speedy
- confidential
- as representative of all employees as possible
- supported by examples

## Ten Questions and Answers
### 1. Who is covered?
The audit could be conducted in a manufacturing plant of, say, 500 employees by a personnel manager working with a middle manager. An employee representative can be included in the team. They will need a 15–20 per cent sample, representative of all employees. The team should be required to report to the board, as commitment from the top of the company is essential in any major employee involvement exercise.

### 2. How long does it take?
Whilst varying, depending on the size of organisation, for the manufacturing unit of 500 employees four days should be allowed to conduct the audit, and a week at most for writing up the report. Any kind of review can stir up feelings of uncertainty amongst employees, so it should be undertaken and reported on quickly.

### 3. What is the first step?
Clear terms of reference should be agreed at board level; for example:

To carry out a short review of employee communications to cover the following principal aspects –

a) The provision of information to all employees about matters that affect their jobs, the way in which they work and their own personal well-being and security;
b) The opportunities presented, and taken, to ascertain people's views, in order to improve the quality of management's decision-making;
c) The way in which parts of the organisation, dependent upon each other, communicate;

d) The effectiveness of other employee communication machinery, including the company appraisal system, reports, house journals, noticeboards, face to face briefings, etc.

## 4. What questions should be asked?
The questions for the interviews with employees should be framed to discover what actually happens within the organisation. The areas covered may include:

- communication
- consultation
- specific management accountability for communicating with and involving employees
- management development and training
- training on communication and provision of information for managers, representatives and employees generally

In a highly unionised organisation management is often alarmed to find that the unions and shop stewards are much more efficient at communicating than supervisory and management staff.

## 5. What should the company tell employees about the review?
Once the terms of reference are decided and the key areas to be covered agreed, employees and employee representatives should be told about the imminent audit by a board director, preferably the chief executive. If this is not done fully and systematically, distrust and rumour will soon develop. Also the audit team will be hampered in their work because some of those they will be interviewing may have developed a negative attitude to the exercise. The communication should stress that the enquiry will concentrate as much on strengths as on weaknesses – it is no management witch-hunt.

## 6. What are the mechanics of a DIY audit?
The audit team should interview the sample individually and in groups. The survey is in essence qualitative rather than quantitative, and the interviews should be semi-structured, using an agreed structure of questions, but not a formal detailed questionnaire. Advice should be taken on framing the questions to be asked, and training given to the audit team on carrying out and interpreting the interviews.

Areas to be probed in, say, our manufacturing firm are the down-the-line, cascade communication from the top, communications across shop floor and offices on operational and administrative issues, and how communications work up from employee representative channels.

In addition, special arrangements may have to be made by the audit team to take account of shifts and continuous processes, units scattered geographically and travelling employees such as sales representatives. Naturally the interviews have to take place on company time. They should be conducted as near the workplace as possible with convenience more important than comfort.

## 7. Isn't it difficult for a member of the company's own management team to do the interviewing?

The choice of the audit team is obviously important. They must be respected by all, be capable, with training, of conducting the interviews – without letting their own opinions show through. They should be people who are better known for their ability rather than their ambition, and be just as credible with managers and employees alike.

## 8. What should the report cover?

The report does not have to be very detailed, although it should comprehensively answer the questions agreed and meet the terms of reference. Its aim is to highlight the main problems, and illustrate this with examples. You will be looking for perhaps two or three broad brush conclusions to guide you. Particular attention should be paid to areas where the company believed it had communicated successfully, and put this against the reality. It may be that the audit team uncovered communications problems not anticipated by the terms of reference, and these will need added amplification.

Some of the findings may well be pretty unpalatable to some – especially the personnel function – and the reassurance of that backing of senior management to the team is important.

## 9. Who should receive the report?

The senior executives of the location covered should receive the report, and some version of it should at least then be made available to all those senior managers whose departments have been audited. How far it goes beyond that will depend on what the report has revealed. The first presentation of key findings should in any case be made by the audit team to the board, and they can then become the arbiters of corporate sensibilities. Ideally, all employees should be given a relevant summary of findings, perhaps in the house journal.

## 10. Who discusses and decides what action should be taken?

The best solution is to set up a joint working party chaired by the chief executive or the personnel director, and comprising representatives of management and employees. Guidelines and good intentions may flow from this, but ultimately it is always the individual manager who has to ensure that communication and involvement are effective within his area of responsibility. The need for management development training is likely to follow, and some very large organisations, like British Airways, on the back of far more sophisticated research than the DIY audit described, develop tailor-made courses to meet their needs. For smaller organisations there are a number of public and private sector training providers who can help, never forgetting local colleges of further education and universities who may develop a course designed to meet your own needs.

## You Can't Change Attitudes Without Changing Behaviour

There is a fond belief – nurtured to some extent by the communications industry – that simply communicating more, communicating better is an end in itself. All the company newspapers, briefing groups, videos, company conferences, employee annual reports and the rest, however, will not lead to the corporate nirvana unless and until something actually happens. That something will either be changes in what people do and how they do it, or changes in people.

All the communication in the world about, say, the need for improved quality or lower absenteeism, is not going to work until cause and effect is established on a clear personal basis – like suppliers or people getting fired for sub-standard quality or timekeeping; like setting higher standards and sticking to them. Good communication can make for much easier acceptance of rational cause and effect, but communication alone will not lead to meaningful change.

The quid pro quo to this is to reward achievers and to explain ad nauseam exactly what the new goals are that all in the organisation must and will achieve. Any hail-fellow-well-met failure from the personnel or PR department can communicate – the tough job has to come from the chief executive and down the operational line-management network. People who are wrong have to be identified and removed – fired or invited to look around. Everyone who remains must know the targets they have been set, upon which they will be judged, and the penalties and benefits of failure or success. They need to know how they are doing, and so do you. They need to know what the basis is for rewarding extra achievement, and so do you.

If your payment system is flat payment based on the lowest common denominator, because it is tidier and easier to negotiate with the unions, then do not be surprised if your call for people to go for gold goes unheeded. An army marches at the pace of its slowest man, and the slowest, least committed man or woman in your organisation will become the yardstick by which others in the section pace themselves. If you believe in free enterprise and competition, why should you think otherwise? Successful companies like ICI, IBM, Ford and Rank Xerox all leave themselves flexibility in their payment systems to reward effort. It is an insult to your better people to pay them the same as the worst. It verges on an insult to your better people to 'communicate' and exhort all to do better if you do not act and weed out the worst. Any fool can treat everyone alike, any coward does. It takes courage to root out passengers and to reward achievers, but the benefits are obvious.

Research and destroy? Research and build. Research findings are not produced for casual interest or simply to communicate. They are there – be it for a brand or a political party – to be used and acted upon. They are there to help make better decisions and to create a climate in which tough decisions can more easily be accepted.

# It Could Never Happen To Us

## Worst Impressions

First impressions matter, but worst impressions will stay in people's memories much longer, and be recalled much more quickly.

There are two main potential causes of worst impressions – your own stupidity or weakness, and your inability to cope well in a crisis.

First, stupidity. Most worst impressions stem from people being caught off-guard, relaxing and becoming informal or over-familiar when common sense (the least common sense of them all) should have warned you off. Drink often has a lot to do with this – impairing judgements and letting the guard slip. A tonic and bitters or white wine and soda is a good idea at formal and most informal gatherings of people with whom you have day to day working relationships. The beer or gin too many can become the catalyst that leads to any number of horrors – the compulsive urge to tell lavatorial jokes, to swearing, to giving your *real* views about 'him' or 'her', to becoming aggressive or pathetically weepy and self-pitying.

Worse still is the temptation to hint at or make unwanted *or* wanted sexual advances with your peers, seniors or juniors. Monogamy may leave a lot to be desired, but few reputations can survive the knowledge or suspicion of a sexual adventurer bubbling away under a calm exterior. In pulp fiction about office romance this may seem fine. The novelettes are now quite racy, keeping up surprisingly with the times. Whereas just a few years ago the big encounter just talked about him crushing her against his tweeds, they now talk a lot more explicitly about who did what to whom. But people are still not ready for the sexual revolution in real life. Real-life sexuality really does still shock people.

The answer, I am afraid, is to take a grip on yourself and make sure you avoid these obvious and avoidable alcoholic and sexual pitfalls. All your hard work in winning people's confidence and respect can be dashed against these well marked reefs. We all *do* remember people at their worst, or at pictures painted of them by others. I have never looked at a dead person for fear that they will blot out happier more attractive images of people I have loved.

Maria Callas was one of the great women of our time, able to stir our passions in every meaning of the word. But I cannot get out of my mind an unflattering Associated Press photograph of her which was front-paged everywhere in November 1955. She had just been served with a summons in her dressing room at the Chicago Opera House by Marshal

Stanley Pringle and Deputy Sheriff Dan Smith after her performance in *Madame Butterfly*. Still in her Cio-Cio-San kimono, she was lost in rage and fury and her snarling, graceless picture came to haunt her and fans like me.

Photographs can and do capture people at their worst or their most foolish. A photograph used by Harold Evans in his book *Pictures on a Page** shows a girl kneeling over her boyfriend on a beach. He had almost died from drowning and a photographer had tried to capture the tragic scene. In fact the girl, looking up and seeing the camera, automatically smiled through years of conditioning to smile at cameras.

More trivially a phrase or image can stick in your mind and get in the way of more rational judgement or enjoyment. If I tell you that all ballerinas have bad feet it will colour your enjoyment of *Swan Lake* the next time you see it. I was told, rightly or wrongly, that Clark Gable had bad breath, and it ruins his films for me, particularly *Gone with the Wind* and his big scene with Vivien Leigh. Then there are certain things you cannot imagine some people ever doing. At a very formal dinner I was attending of shipping people aboard a Norwegian liner docked in England, the chairman proposed the loyal toast as 'The Queen of England coupled with the King of Norway'. Rather like the newspaper headline that screamed 'Home Secretary to Act on Porn Videos', it creates a lasting image in the mind you could well do without. Don't let that happen to you.

Also, always behave and speak as though even people you think you should be able to trust will, instead, spread gossip about you. Everyone loves a secret, a confidence, but just as nature conspires against a vacuum so human nature conspires against confidences. The Royal visit to China in October 1986 was nearly ruined by off-the-cuff comments reportedly made by Prince Philip to British students there about parts of China being 'ghastly', and the risk the students ran of getting 'slitty eyes'. I always work on the basis that it is unfair to tell anybody secrets. You can tell them confidential things they need to know, but confiding in people things they do not need to know seems to me a sign of weakness in yourself and an unfair burden on the other party. It is, in fact, one of the crudest ways of trying to win friendship and acceptance.

When I was with the CBI I was telephoned by an overseas agency with a piece of information which seemed to be of the most extreme international importance. They used it as an inducement to meet me. I smelled an entrapment and acted accordingly, passing on the details to the Foreign Office. But for the few days I carried that secret around with me, I felt I would burst – wanting to tell everyone I met to show how important I was. In fact I did just that eventually, once I knew it was safe to do so, and used the material as the basis for my spy novel, *Seward's Folly*.

*William Heinemann, London, 1978

This leads on to the second area of worst impressions. Had I not used my common sense and met those people, I could have had a difficult time extricating myself from the mess later. Worst of all, my judgement in agreeing to meet them would have clearly been unsound – and if it is unsound under pressure, would I be the sort of person to continue in high office?

A crisis of any kind can show the worst or best of people – normally one extreme or the other – and we will always remember that extreme. In the home, a small fire, a suspected burglar downstairs, a medical crisis – someone choking, fainting, needing mouth-to-mouth – in these unplanned, unrehearsed emergencies all your veneer of urbanity may be stripped away, and you might act like a coward or panic. Somerset Maugham caught just such a moment perfectly in his short story 'The Door of Opportunity'.

That story was fiction. Fact at first hand can be very disturbing. In a bank one day a man collapsed in the queue in front of me with what seemed like a heart attack. Fortunately another man in the queue had St John's training and very professionally went about the energetic thumping and cardiac massage necessary to get the lungs moving – including the very loud and obvious breaking of the ribs in this case. I hovered about offering to give any assistance possible. Mouth-to-mouth was being administered and the man had vomited, so I was relieved when none was asked. The victim's friend in the queue however went to pieces, threatening our Good Samaritan with law suits and jail if the man died, yelling and generally getting in the way until the ambulance arrived. He was in his late middle-age and dressed well, clearly 'a boss' of some kind. Had his staff and employers seen him then, however, they would never have viewed him in the same light, however good or popular he was before. Wartime crises like this, of course, were commonplace.

As a leader you must set the tone. At the time of the blitz in London, research suggested that children were not really afraid of the bangs, flashes and shudders from the bombs. Two factors had a much greater bearing – separation from their mother, and the relative anxiety communicated by the mother. If she was calm, so was her child.

Panic attacks are suffered by over three per cent of people, and all of us on occasions have felt our nerves get the better of us. Symptoms range from blushing and blotchy necks and sweatiness, to palpitations, red spots before the eyes, ringing in the ears, vomiting, uncontrollable weeping/grizzling, loss of control of the bowels and bladder, and possibly blackouts. All hardly things which will impress those around you of your leadership qualities.

Those suffering from severe panic attack should seek therapy, for their own sake and those of others around them. The rest of us should be able to help ourselves by a mixture of things – more preparation and rehearsal, desensitising ourselves from the fear by deliberately exposing ourselves to it (getting back on the horse that threw you; overcoming the fear of flying by understanding more about planes and their procedures, why they fly, what the different engine noises mean, and flying more knowledgeably), and by being a positive rather than negative thinker of the things which *will* go right not which *may* go wrong. Ask yourself what is so special about *you* that you think terrible things might happen to you, or that people will be staring at you or even notice you. I am self-conscious about wearing a hat. When I do, if a punk stands next to me in the tube with lime green hair cut in a Mohican style, sporting a safety pin through his nose, I still feel people are staring at *me*. If at a match you are convinced that rugby players in a scrum are all talking about *you*, if you go round telling yourself that just because you've been diagnosed paranoid it doesn't mean to say they are *not* all after you – then don't be surprised if you have trouble coping with panic. Try laughing at yourself. You'll probably be the only one who does.

Crises at work can and do occur from time to time, and most of them can and should be predicted. Some, like bank hold-ups, are the subject of well-rehearsed procedure ('bandits' at xyz bank, High Street seems to be the marvellously simple message given by staff reporting a raid taking place). Fire drills and the other emergency procedures for certain industries with special needs – the chemical, petroleum, nuclear and airline industries, for instance – are all common enough routines. But crises can hit anyone. Over the last fifteen years I have been perhaps uniquely involved with major emergencies ranging from the three-day week brought on by the Heath/NUM confrontation; terrorist threats against my person which necessitated Special Branch protection; looking after the public relations side of the Laker collapse for the UK travel industry; health scares including Legionnaire's Disease; road, sea and air crashes involving fatalities; substantial redundancy announce-ments and factory closures which ran the risk of strike action; negotiation with network TV investigative consumer and current affairs teams; product recalls; receivership announcements; and involvement in major takeover situations, from both sides of the fence. Crises are stressful and can be very upsetting on a personal basis. Curiously though, and a little shamefully, they can also be very satisfying, making you feel important for once, and at the centre of things. Whatever your motivations, however, you must try and react positively.

## Reacting Positively in a Crisis

Organisations can have any number of catastrophes which can threaten their prosperity and even survival. There can be unexpected new taxes or trade bans, product recalls on safety grounds, product blackmail by criminals and extreme lobbies on, say, animal liberation, damaging consumerist reports on TV or in the press, a strike, the need to announce major redundancies, a scandal involving your senior management, a health problem in a plant, a hostile takeover bid, the defection of key management to your competitors, a technological breakthrough in your sector which leaves you stranded – as happened with the traditional Swiss watch industry – and so on.

Nobody wants a crisis, but it is possible, indeed it is the duty of management to try to minimise potential damage and to leave the organisation's corporate image unscathed, or in certain circumstances even improved.

There are three basic principles to follow when dealing with a major bad news crisis.

You must deal with it with honesty.

With efficiency.

And with people who have had experience of major *news* crises before. A crisis is no time to find yourself on a learning curve.

First, honesty, I am not talking about whether you should lie or not. If you want to lie, hide and deceive, then we are in the realms of Joseph Goebbels-style propaganda and lawsuits.

Of course, you don't lie. But the fact is that you will know more than the media, more than MPs, more than the trade unions about the real truth behind the crisis. The real question you will be asking yourself is how much of the truth do you tell, and when?

Never let yourself be railroaded into saying too much too soon. A useful tactic is to issue a statement to the media saying you are still assessing the situation and expect to be in a position to issue more information by whenever you think reasonable. This will buy you a little time.

As a generalisation, full disclosure of the facts, if properly handled, is the best advice. If the story is bad, you will at least come out as honest. Also you will hopefully be a one-day wonder and not a drawn-out constant source of tit-bits, new revelations and rumours.

If you have some latitude on when to issue your 'bad news' statement, putting it out early evening on a Friday could mean you fail to make the light Saturday national papers and may also miss the Sundays. Come Monday you *may* have been overtaken by events. If there is another major news story breaking – a Royal Wedding, the Budget, an assassination attempt on the Pope or a leading Western political leader, then again the amount of room for you in the printed and broadcast media could be mercifully little. Don't try and be too cute in this respect however. Remember you want to come out of this as efficient and honest, not as some sharp media manipulating spiv.

But never forget the constraints imposed upon you by your insurers and lawyers. Under no circumstances should anything be said by an employee of the company, or anyone speaking on behalf of the company, which might amount to an admission that the accident had been caused or contributed to by some fault on the part of the organisation, its employees, agents or suppliers. You need to establish now with your insurers what action you may take without reference to them in an emergency, and what will require specific authority.

Being honest and as open as possible is a first requisite, coupled with the need to be as speedy as you can. This leads on to the equal need for efficiency.

Good intentions, however genuine, are nothing like enough. If the story breaks at four o'clock on a Friday afternoon, you can't call a board meeting, issue a committee written statement late in the evening and expect to see your good intentions reflected by the media. Equally, you can't push an inexperienced 'company spokesman' on the radio or TV, or at a hastily called and badly run press conference, and achieve a fair representation of your situation in the media.

Even if you think you're pretty good and confident with your press contacts, then you are in for a shock. What you will more than likely find is that the story is a news-desk story, being put together by whoever the news editor has available to put on it when it breaks.

You might reckon you know the national media people of importance to your sector – they may be motoring correspondents, food writers, personal finance writers, gardening editors, whoever . . . But if the story breaks as a *news* story then it will be a whole new team of people working furiously to very tight deadlines, who know little or nothing about you – other than whatever may be lurking in their library cuttings files – and who probably won't have the time, nor inclination, even to contact their own specialist writers on your sector (they are probably hardly ever in the office anyway); or if it's TV their current affairs teams, even if they have just done a programme on your industry.

And it gets worse. These news-desk people won't seem at all like that friendly specialist writer you may have had a long lunch with a few months earlier. He or she will be very direct, will either ask you probing questions at the very heart of the matter or make assumptions which show complete ignorance of how your business operates. They will be in a hurry, will brusquely cut short any flannel, and if they don't think they are getting anywhere with you will probably demand to speak to your chairman or MD. They will have your annual report in front of them, and may already have a couple of lines out to one of your non-execs somebody at the paper knows.

You will interpret this as rudeness, as an insult, but it isn't. The journalist understands the limitations on you to speak, and simply wants to get a speedy answer to his questions from someone. Remember that the main motivations of any journalist in this situation are twofold. First, he or she has to make very sure they get at least as much of the story as their competitors. If not they will be in real trouble with their editor. Secondly, what they really want of course is to find either a new angle to the story or to unearth more information than their competitors. All this does not necessarily mean that they want to do you down or just generate 'bad news' headlines. Most journalists are just as happy with a story about 'this is what went wrong, this is how we are solving it'. Consumerist writers also like 'victories', good news – that is 'we spotted this problem, raised it and we are pleased to say that thanks to us the firm has now put it right'.

One problem, however, can be newspaper headline-writers. However positive the story as filed by the journalist, it may well be cut down by the sub-editor, and your nice comment lost for ever; and, worse still, through no fault of the journalist, some terrible cataclysmic headline may be composed which catches the reader's eye, but does not necessarily reflect the tone of the article. Like the common cold, there is no known cure for this.

Your chairman or MD will need advice. Should he talk to the media at all? Should he go 'off-record' perhaps, whatever he thinks that means, or 'non-attributable' – whatever he thinks that means. What line should he take? Should he appear on TV? Has he been trained in TV techniques? If not, can a training session be arranged within a couple of hours?

## Emergency Procedures Plan

What this scenario highlights is the need for virtually any organisation to draw up an emergency procedures plan, not unlike those which more obviously exposed industries like transportation/aviation/chemicals have as a matter of course.

In, say, a typical manufacturing company a working party should be convened by the chief executive and given the job of drawing up an emergency procedures plan. The group might include someone from personnel (access to personnel records may be necessary in emergencies); from production (safety or quality issues); the company secretary to deal with legal issues; the office services manager (word processors, telexes, computers all may need to be accessed); and marketing (suppliers may need to be contacted – if it is some kind of poison threat the bar codes and sell-by dates and any on-pack information may help isolate those items which may need taking off-shelf).

The group must decide a duty roster, who would form the emergency panel, and who would be team leader. A small card – credit card size – should be produced giving all relevant home numbers. This should be carried at all times. If the industry is a sensitive one, the team leader should be expected to carry a bleeper at all times by which he or she could be summoned. The team leader should be on the board.

The next requirement is a company document setting out procedures. An incident report form should be drawn up, which should be used as soon after the incident as possible by everyone involved, to log events and action taken.

Problems frequently happen at night, at weekends and during holidays. One of the first requirements will be to set up an operations room, and this will need full administrative and secretarial support facilities – the switchboard will need manning and special lines dedicated to the incident room (during a big crisis an ordinary board will be swamped); typists will be required along with access to electronically stored data; refreshments and petty cash may be called upon; keys to locked departments and storage areas may be needed. The operations room may well be open for twenty-four hours a day, and so staff replacements will be needed.

One person should be the sole media contact and he or she should make a log of all calls: the time, name of journalist, and drift of what was said. Others may be permitted to read out an agreed statement, but not to comment in any way beyond it. Although only one person should at any time be the media contact and interviewee, two or three in the organisation, including the chief executive, should be trained and coached on press, radio and TV role-playing in a number of 'worst possible' scenarios. One tip, if press calls are really inundating you, is to ask the Press Association to nominate a reporter to cover your story, and to refer the media calls to PA.

If there have been deaths or injuries and there is public concern, you or the emergency services – probably the police – should consider issuing a telephone number for worried people to contact. Remember that with TV and especially local radio, the media is now instant. Decide on a number and it could be on TV and radio within the half hour, and ringing.

Under no circumstances should the names of people killed or injured be given out until next of kin have been informed. It is advisable to ask for the help of the police when face to face notification of next of kin is necessary. The Back Hall Inspector at New Scotland Yard, on duty twenty-four hours a day, may help in contacting local police stations on your behalf. Where there are fatalities, be prepared for the publicity to reopen after each inquest, when the coroner may choose to comment.

Other important people to explain your situation to in due course are your own employees, especially the salesforce who are on the road and being asked, and retailers and suppliers, whose confidence you need. Phone calls to key accounts by the sales or marketing director will help, possibly a letter to all retailers, certainly a well-positioned comment in the next trade press.

Accidents and crises can happen to anyone, and the bad luck gets worse if it damages your standing with your end customer – the public. Always consider therefore whether you can legitimately broaden the issue of what has happened to you into an industry issue, even a national issue, to deflect some of the flak from yourself. Your trade association, a government department, the adequacy or otherwise of national safety or testing regulations, the World Health Organisation. When it becomes an industry-wide issue, then the damage to your company or brand will be lessened – it could have happened to any of your competitors, that's the message you want. You may even go on the attack and call for higher national standards in this or that, a change in the law. Consider briefing your local MP to see if he agrees with you. He or she might make a statement, write to the minister, table a parliamentary question, go for an adjournment debate.

## Dirty Tricks

In a competitive world, one organisation's crisis can be another's delight, and it is not unknown for competitors to take steps to initiate or escalate your problems. City editors in particular have had to get used to 'no names no pack drill' telephone calls with bits of news, and to receiving unsigned, unmarked information through the mail which may or may not be accurate, but which is always mischievous.

Whether it be competitors, crooks, cranks, or disgruntled employees, check out people on the telephone or who call in person. Ring newspaper switchboards back and reassure yourself who the person asking you these searching questions really is.

Disasters are often visual and so expect press photographers and TV cameras to appear, quite possibly by helicopter. Consider whether to make available picture-taking facilities if you feel it might better be controlled that way. Always remember, however, that if you permit journalists on to your property, you can *beforehand* make clear what you are inviting them to discuss and make it equally clear if there are any confidential new products or secret processes which they may see but which they may not report upon. In certain circumstances you can ask your lawyers to draw up a standard agreement letter to protect you, and only let the journalists in if they agree to sign.

As ever, don't be frivolous in this respect, but do exercise your rights forcefully if you need to. Most journalists will respect them. If you are being asked on to a TV or radio programme, for instance, you have every right to know whether it will be live, whether you will be interviewed alone or as part of a panel, and if the latter who else has been asked. You can also ask for, but maybe will not receive, an indication of the questions which will be put to you. If the interview is to be recorded, and edited later, you can record your own full interview yourself – for use if needed subsequently to complain and win redress should you believe the editing to have been unfair. Monitor what is being said about you generally; monitor Press Association reports (you can access them on viewdata systems) which will be regurgitated all round the country – ask to have them corrected if you think they are wrong in fact or even emphasis.

Finally, just as you occasionally call a fire alarm or bomb alert to make sure procedures are understood and operate smoothly, from time to time convene the emergency panel, perhaps on a Saturday or Sunday, and see if the system works. When another organisation faces the kind of crisis that could have hit you, analyse how they cope and use it as a case history for yourself. Once the real crisis has lulled by all means contact the firm and ask their advice, learn from their experience – most companies are more than happy to share their knowledge on matters of this kind.

## Outsiders In

Self-improvement, self-management is the most effective and most satisfying way forward. Our Twenty Per Cent Factor is generally achievable in most areas of personal and corporate life by an effort to evaluate ourselves, others and situations, and by taking more effective action. As Peter Drucker demonstrated in his book *The Effective Executive**, only effectiveness converts the resources of intelligence, imagination and knowledge into results. And effectiveness can be learned by self-study and improvement, by reading and by analysing the daily examples of cause and effect at home and at work.

One lesson which must be learned early, however, is to know when you need help. A friend of mine – a workaholic – told me that his father once solemnly drove him to the side of a road which gave a good view of a huge cemetery. 'Son,' he said, 'that graveyard is full of people who thought their businesses couldn't survive without them. You can find a list of them in the Yellow Pages.'

The sign of a true expert is their ready acknowledgement that there are other specialists who know more than they do. For businesses the most common counselling and support retained – outside accountancy and legal services – are general management and marketing consultants, such as public relations firms, design houses, advertising agencies, etc.

Professional consultants have had a bad press over the years. It stems back to the cold and clinical image of the 'company doctor' and lingers in the resentment felt by many on the client side towards the high salaries, multi-million pound capitalisations and, above all, the ear and influence that the best consultancies achieve at the highest level.

Consultants. People who steal your watch and charge to tell you the time.

Consultants. People who show up after the battle to bayonet the wounded – probably on their own side.

Consultants. People like rhinoceroses: thick-skinned and charge a lot.

Consultants. All *éminence grise* and no elbow grease.

More than occasionally, however, they can see the wood from the trees and can effect change *because* of their arm's-length relationship, perhaps just one step ahead of those other consultants – receivers.

*William Heinemann, London, 1967

Working with consultants for the first time can be quite traumatic. For some, the very act of asking in consultants – or having consultants imposed upon them – seems like an admission of failure. For some, treating consultants as peers and allies rather than as some kind of service industry equivalent of a foot-in-the-door brush salesman seems difficult. For some, the offer of good objective advice seems an impertinence.

Read these personal diary entries of a fictional 'marketing man' who has suddenly been confronted with PR consultants and a design agency. Our hero's name is Nigel Binkerton-Smythe (created by Richard Gaunt, MD of PR Solutions Ltd). For each occasion you think 'that reaction/ situation rings a bell', award yourself/your organisation one black mark. If by the end you have logged six black marks or more, then your chances of building a positive client/consultancy relationship are slender.

(The most brilliant full-scale satire on the advertising and PR world I have found is J. B. Priestley's novel, *The Image Men*. Originally published in two volumes as *Out of Town* and *London End*, it is a marvellously perceptive work which follows the fortunes of two old scholars – Professor Cosmo Saltana and Dr Owen Tuby – as they set up their Institute of Social Imagistics. They deal with 'over-images', 'under-images', 'emergent images', 'frayed images' (all invented by themselves) and lampoon the worlds of business, politics, further education and the media so well that there are real lessons to be learned from it by us all. Do read it.)

**Entry: 7 February**

Dear Diary,

We had a presentation thing today from some PR people – Bodgers in Sales has taken them on, decided we needed more clout in the trade press.

I must say they were jolly impressive at first – all double-breasted suits and red ties, and just a hint of eau de cologne – and they had put everything they wanted to say on slides so we could actually see what they'd said after they'd said it.

They started by saying they knew we'd invited them in because we wanted more press coverage, but we ought to realise that PR was a bit more complicated than that you know, and banged on about marketing objectives, employee awareness and the need for something called a 'total commitment for integrated communications'.

I could see JB beginning to glaze over and someone said 'tell that to Nigel Dempster' and everyone laughed, and that seemed to wake him up.

Then this university wonder from the agency stood up and said the PR programme was a non-starter until the company had a cohesive marketing policy.

Of course I saw his little game immediately . 'Look here,' I said! 'With great respect, I think you should concentrate on your job, which is to get as much free advertising as you can, and leave marketing to me. It so happens,' I thundered, 'that the board of directors, who have considerably more experience of these matters than you, are more likely to be impressed with a few more column inches than your impertinent views about the impact on our distributors of my new direct-sell discount policy. In any case,' I added, 'that sort of thing is looked after by sales and is nothing to do with the marketing department.'

I can tell you, his face looked a picture. Talk about one up to me! Still, if these agencies employ people without the slightest experience of the real world of marketing, what can they expect.

Anyway, then things began to get a bit nasty. They said that they'd done a 'communications audit' by talking to staff and customers, which I thought was a bit cheeky, and that they thought we had an identity problem. According to them, and this made me laugh, hardly anyone has heard of us and those that have think we still just make corset fasteners – when everyone knows we are one of the biggest widget pressers hereabouts.

Apparently our name does not really describe what we do now, especially after our strategic diversification into coal merchanting. But as JB said, 'If it was good enough for the founder, it's good enough for me, and in any case, our customers know us, have done for years, and that's all that matters.'

I would have thought these people would have begun to take the hint by then, but they carried on.

They said that any form of PR activity would be useless without a thorough organisational review to 'clarify lines of communication internally and externally' or something like that, but Snelling from Personnel put them firmly in their place by saying since when had personnel management been in the realm of public relations? 'After all,' he said, 'look what happens at ACAS.' One up to him, I thought.

Parkinson said that sometimes at drinks parties it was a bit of a rigmarole explaining who he worked for and what he did for a living, and JB said he'd also been wondering that for years. Everyone laughed and JB had that twinkle in his eye. He certainly doesn't show his age.

Well, after that it was plain sailing. They did say something about developing continuing links with the press and especially not regarding the press as a vehicle for free advertising and then clamming up when the heat was on from the media.    JB put them right on that straight away however, explaining that when the press got on to us we always say it's a trade association matter and put them on to the National Federation.    Since the National Federation always refuses to comment on the grounds that it would have to consult the entire membership this, as JB graphically put it, 'has the commie buggers practically snookered from the start.'

That seemed to be the end of the meeting.    JB said we needed to go very carefully, in view of what he called 'the need to proceed at a pace at which the slowest could accept change' - rather a neat phrase I thought.    Anyway everyone agreed, so we left it that the PR people would keep a general eye on things, but not actually **do** anything without consulting JB.

On the other hand, there **was** that exhibition coming up, so perhaps they could do a handout, just for the trade press.    Show the flag a bit.


## Entry:   2 March

You remember I mentioned the trade exhibition the other day?    Well, JB has asked me to take charge of it!

I asked the PR people if they knew anything about widget exhibitions and they said no, only the Motor Show, the Boat Show and the Information Technology Exhibition, and I thought if they think we can spend that sort of money on WIDGETEX '88 they had better think again, and I told them I'd let them know.

In the end I got Daphne to design a stand, as she's really jolly clever and did a wonderful job with the decorations for the tennis club Hallowe'en social. She's come up with a theme of WITCH WIDGET? with our entire range stuck in the twigs of broomsticks set against a black background with lots of coloured stars and moons.    She did a little model in a shoebox and it looks really super.

The PR people were a bit long-faced when I showed it to them.    Still, it does them good to see they don't have a monopoly on creativity all the time.    One of them said;    'Why don't you have lots of ghosts and Draculas and vampires handing out literature and scare the pants off the punters?', which shows they can be constructive even in defeat.

Then they showed me their ideas for the press kit and I must say I was a bit disappointed.    It was all very factual and technical and the releases   hardly mentioned us at all.

So I made them put our name in every sentence and peppered it with a few phrases like 'England's number one widget manufacturer' and 'Probably the best widgets in the world'.    That's what we  need, fighting talk, if we're going to get out of the recession.

They said it was hardly objective and I had to remind them sharply that we weren't here to be objective, but to sell widgets.    It just goes to show that this PR game is a piece of cake really.    With my flair for publicity growing by the minute I can fast see the day approaching when we won't need **them** any more.    I sometimes wonder what they do for their £3,000 a month retainer.    I might just tell them we have to sell something like 12,000 widgets just to pay their fee, but on the other hand I might not, as JB gets very hairy if you so much as mention profit margins outside The Sanctum.


## Entry:   8 May

WIDGETEX '88 turned out to be a bit of a low-key affair.    Our stand was at the back near the gents and everyone we tried to accost said 'Must rush old boy' and dived into the loos, despite the enthusiastic attentions of our very realistic ghosts, ghouls and vampires.

As usual Greatco stole the limelight with a flashy stand - rather tasteless to my mind - right near the entrance with lots of lights and television screens, the whole caboodle presided over by a gaggle of over-endowed giggling girls they called the Widgettes.

When I told the chap our PR agency sent over to look after the media hordes that I was surprised people were impressed by that sort of thing nowadays, he turned purple and said something about 'bloody amateurs,' and I must say I agree with him entirely.

I told the agency to make sure we got a better site next year, if there **is** a next year, I added darkly. I think they are beginning to get the message.

During the week David Green-Lovegrove from Greatco came over to the stand, all suede shoes and teeth, and invited me over for a drink saying, 'Perhaps you'd like to see how it really should be done.' As if we have anything to learn from Greatco. I said if I wanted to play Space Invaders I could go to the pub. That put him in his place and no mistake. The man is a viper.

## Entry: 4 June

The PR people seem to have been plotting behind my back. Apparently someone took all this corporate identity stuff at the board presentation seriously and the next thing I know we've agreed to have ourselves put under the microscope by some sort of design agency. What design has to do with marketing is anyone's guess. After all, what can an art school drop-out know of the widget business? I just know they're in cahoots with the PR agency, probably in bed with them financially I wouldn't wonder.

They sent their top chap to interview me. Apparently he'd designed stations on the French Underground. I ask you! He wanted to know how I saw the company, so I said all the usual stuff from the annual report about forward thinking, dynamic, thrusting, towards the year 2000, progress through partnership, all that sort of thing, and I know I impressed him as he went very quiet indeed.

Then he asked me about marketing plans, market share and whether we'd ever done any market research.

I told him quite firmly that all that kind of thing was absolutely confidential and there was no possibility whatever of my discussing company strategy with some nosey consultant.

I could tell by then that I was on top, so I judged the moment right to give him a piece of my mind. 'Look here,' I said, 'if you think you can come in here, paint everything pretty colours, give us a new symbol and then go away congratulating yourself that you've contributed something to this company, then you can jolly well forget it.

'You tell me,' I said, pressing my point home, 'how many extra widgets will we sell as a result of all this nonsense?'

Well, of course, he was stumped. I'd got his Achilles heel. Then I played my trump card. 'In any case,' I said, 'we've already got a new design scheme for the company going through at the moment.' And I flipped him through Daphne's designs for the staff Christmas Dinner and Dance invitations and menus, the ones which show the herald pointing to the horizon wearing a winged helmet and a tabard depicting the activities of the company's various divisions.

After that, as you can imagine, he was a bit sheepish. He said he didn't seem to be getting very far so he upped and went.

He's now probably cruising round Covent Garden as I write thinking up ideas for rude murals. Stick to what you know about, say I, and leave marketing to the professionals.

## Garbage In – Garbage Out

The way to find the best PR consultancy, advertising agency, sales promotion company or design house is to ask around and look around – find out who did the work you respect.

Know what you want – what you want from other people. And what these 'other people' in the consultancy would want from *you* is a full briefing and clear objectives. If you are not reasonably sure of what you do want then it is too early to look to consultants to help. If you cannot give a good brief then, to borrow from computer jargon, you will be facing a situation of garbage in – garbage out.

The jury is still out on whether a *heavy* dependence on consultancy staff – either at arm's length or as implants working alongside you – is a good or bad idea. I have heard it argued by general management consultants that even having consultants head up-line functions – like finance and marketing – can make more sense than having your own people do it. The extra marginal cost of fees relative to in-house salaries is probably insignificant when set alongside the benefit which truly top and committed consultancy talent can bring to the business. As for the use generally of PR, design, sales promotions and ad agencies, the verdict was reached before the war in the USA, and since the 1950s in the UK, that well-selected, well-briefed external support is a wise investment for most organisations. But make them feel an important part of the team. And if at times they seem like prima donnas, then remember you probably can't make top 'C' without them. The more mature the client, in my experience, the more respect with which they treat the consultancy team and the better work they get.

The advertising world is less dogged by this, partly because of the high budgets, partly because of the apparent science of the attendant media buying, media evaluation and research techniques. Even though some advertisers put media buying out to an independent media agency and/or make their main agency work for fees rather than the typical fifteen per cent commission on advertising revenue placed, nobody with any sense even contemplates doing their own creative work. They use either established agencies or respected 'hot shops'. All this despite the propensity of us all to have bright ideas in the bath. Like the football referee, being an advertising agent means doing a job everyone thinks they can do better, and on which everyone is a bar-room expert.

Consultants can often spot your business's and brand's Twenty Per Cent Factor more easily than you can. They have done it many times before. Insist on the best team for your needs. Lean on them. Trust them. The success will be yours.

# The Twenty Per Cent Factor: From Coué to Carnegie

Identifying your areas of potential and weakness and working *steadily* towards self-improvement has been my main theme – The Twenty Per Cent Factor. Turning this awareness into action, with practical guidance on how to do it, has been our parallel theme.

As important as learning has been our need to 'unlearn' some of the influences of the past quarter of a century – the blind worship and attempted emulation of the *images* we have of heroes from the worlds of business and entertainment; the 1960s attempts to canonise the importance of individuality and to exercise an almost constitutional right to self-expression; the 'go for gold'/'go for it' mentality glibly promoted by the talented, privileged or lucky few.

In their place I have throughout this book advocated sets of values which were commonly accepted before the last war, values to which a new generation has never been fairly exposed, and against which my own has been poisoned. Values which include the study of others, the sublimation of some of our individuality, the use of self-interested servility, and the embracement of unfashionable clichés like 'the customer is always right' and 'do to others as you would have them do to you'. I believe the advice I have given can quickly lead to a much greater sense of fulfilment, the achievement of sensible goals and the redis-covery of fun and happiness in personal and corporate life to replace the designer boredom and cynicism of the 1980s. Much of the unhappiness we see around us arises from feelings of failure and rejection by people exposed to images of apparent success on TV, in magazines and other media, of smiling, self-satisfied 'winners', arrivistes and parvenus.

By improving ourselves by twenty per cent, by reaching this attainable new plateau, and then after a while by ratcheting up a further twenty, and then later another twenty, we too can become winners by our own and anybody else's definition.

My advice to reject much of today's accepted wisdom seems radical. It does seem radical to reject the cult of individualism for conformity. It does seem radical to counsel against copying business superstars – pursuing excellence and going for the 'burn'. The fact is, however, that none of this is the least bit radical. Quite the reverse – until recently it was conventional thinking. Conventional thinking with deep roots in philosophy and practical application. The real shock to me is how rapidly and thoroughly these self-evident truths became discredited following that now discredited decade of the 1960s.

Three very different examples follow of what for most of this century has been – and to me still remains – valuable conventional thinking: James, Coué and Carnegie.

Psychologist and philosopher William James was one of the founders of pragmatism and, incidentally, the brother of novelist and essayist Henry James. Initially trained as a doctor, he later turned from physiology to psychology and philosophy, initially drawing from Darwin, emphasising the complementary functioning of both the biological and philosophical side of the mind. He went on to argue what lies at the heart of The Twenty Per Cent Factor – that we make use of only a small part of our physical and mental resources, that we live far within our limits.

From the same era, the turn of the nineteenth century, came another medically trained man who also made the link between the natural sciences and philosophy. Frenchman Emile Coué, a pharmacist, developed a theory of healing based on auto-suggestion – 'Self-Mastery Through Conscious Auto-Suggestion'. He lectured in Canada and the USA towards the end of his life in 1922 and 1923, when his system had become known as Couéism.

Couéism gave us one of the sickliest sounding pieces of advice of all time, and it jars today more than ever before. Yet it is another cliché that we ignore to our cost. Coué taught his patients to think and say to themselves over and over again – 'Every day in every way, I am getting better and better'. Try saying that out loud today in the pub or in the works canteen and you would be ridiculed.

Steady, measured self-improvement is far from ridiculous however. Believe you can get a little better, believe in The Twenty Per Cent Factor – but don't say it out loud. You don't need a soapbox to win conviction. Private conviction is what works. We are our own hardest taskmasters. We are our own cathedrals. We can ask and expect more of ourselves than anyone else.

Ten years after the death of Coué came the publication of one of the most influential popular books of this century, a seminal work in the area of applied human relations and one never bettered. It is *How to Win Friends and Influence People*, written by Dale Carnegie. Carnegie was driven to write the book following a survey conducted by the University of Chicago and the United YMCA Schools. It asked the people of a typical American town – Meriden, Connecticut – about themselves, what interested them and what subject areas they would most like to study. Health was the first unsurprising choice for the adults in the survey. Little change there with today, and little change on their second choice. It was how to understand and get on better with people.

Surprisingly, there was no practical textbook covering this subject and Dale Carnegie decided to write his own to use on his courses. This desire to improve ourselves and to improve our relations with others is just as strong today as in the days of Coué and Carnegie.

The myth of the overnight sensation, of suddenly bursting from a chrysalis, of striking it rich, getting lucky, has surely been discredited by experience. The only sure way of making money out of gold prospecting is to sell picks and pans to the hopefuls. Waiting for your luck to change in life is a loser's easy way out – when it does not arrive just blame Lady Luck, not yourself.

Most successful people – people on the national scene or in your own circle of acquaintances – have taken years to get there, years to develop their presentational and inter-personal skills. We notice them *arriving* – we tend to forget how long it took for them to get there.

Success on its many levels – personal and corporate – is in our own hands. Improve your understanding and performance in the ways described and take up that first twenty per cent. It will not only help you achieve a greater degree of success, it can be the key to some things which success and fulfilment are really about, but which remain as elusive as ever to some of the be-knighted, ennobled and fawned over stars of business, entertainment and politics. The small matters of contentment, self-respect and happiness.

Only fools and geniuses look for overnight success, and most of us are neither.

# Index

Absenteeism, 84,140
Accents/dialect, 47–8
Advertising, 8,81–3
    passim,95, 106–8,110,
    114–16 passim,119,
    129,130,151,155
Aggression, 73
Appearance, 28,30–6
Architecture, 5,98–101
Argyle, Michael, 37,43
Aristotle, 52
Arkwright, Richard, 13
Assessment analyses,
    16–23,26,75–6,89–91
Audits, 131,134–9
Australia, 40
Award schemes, 102

Bankruptcies, 24–5
Banks, 83,97–9 passim
Barnett, Corelli, 59
Beatles, 10,11
Beeton's Dictionary, 49
Bentham, Jeremy, 53
Berger, Dr Walter, 28
Berne, Dr Eric, 15,130
'Bingo' war, 116
Body language, 37–40
Brands, 106–16,130; own
    label, 110
Branson, Richard,
    80,118,119
Briefing Groups, 85–6,88
British Airways, 84,106,107,
    118–20 passim, 139
British Association of
    Industrial Editors, 95
Budgeting, 66–7
Burke, Edmund, 88
Burton, Sir Richard, 33

Capote, Truman, 29
Carlyle, Thomas, 44
Carnegie, Dale, 159
CBI, 46,124,127,142
Clark, Lord, 81,99
Class, 43,47–8,63
Communication, 9,
    62–76,132–7; internal,
    84–6,94–7,135–9
Competition,
    27,54,58,114,128, 129,149;
    internal, 29
Conscience, 53–6
Consultants, 5,74,84,109–10,
    150–5

Corporate style, 102–3
Cosmetic surgery, 33–4
Coué, Emile, 159
Craniology, 32
Creativity, 117–24
Crises, 143–50
Criticism, 73
Cryptic colouration, 34,36
Customers,
    8,9,11,27,44,56,72,
    74,78,80–4
    passim,99,100,102,
    109,120,128,129,134–5

Darwin, Charles,
    32,34,36,159
Design, corporate, 101;
    interior, 5, 98–101
Dinner parties, 42–3
Direct mail, 115
Dirty tricks, 149–50
Discipline, 92–3
Discretion, 142,145
Divorce, 51
Doyle, Prof Peter, 66
Dress, 5,11,35–6
Drink, 42,141
Drucker, Peter, 150

Edwardes, Sir Michael,
    15,86
Emergencies, 143–4,147–9
Emerson, Ralph Waldo, 57
Empathy, 36–48 passim
Empiricism, 53,55
Employees, 9,27,73,78,83–6,
    94–7,127,129,135–9
Employers/bosses, 11,
    13–14,27, 41–7,
    54–6,61,80,94,102 see also
    Management
Encoding, 39
Equality, racial/sexual, 48
Evans, Harold, 142
Eye contact, 31,40
Eyton, Audrey, 108

Face, 31–4
Fixation, 73,74
Follet, Mary Parker, 72
Frustration, 74

Galton, Sir Francis, 32
Game Plan, 89–91
Garnett, John, 69,85

Germany, 35,54,60,79
Gordon, W. J. J., 118
Group approach, 29,30,132

Hair, 34–6 passim
Hall tests, 132
Handshakes, 45
Henderson, Monika, 43
Hess, Prof Eckhard, 31
Holder and Scorah, 51
Home life, 41–4
Honesty, 145–6
Hovland, C. I., 75
Hume, David, 53

Image, 62,78–83,
    98–103,151, 156
Individualism, cult of,
    10–11,156
Industrial relations, 86 see
    also Strikes
Industrial Society, 69,85
Innovation, product, 110–11,
    117–20
Integrity, 56–8

James, William, 159
Japan/Japanese,
    33,39,58,66–7,
    73,79,81,84,128
Job satisfaction, 69,84
Journalists, 111,113–14,
    146–7, 149
Journals, house, 95–6

Kalven, Harry, 30
Kant, Immanuel, 53,55,65–6
Korn/Ferry, 62

Languages, 38
Lavater, Jonathan Kaspar,
    32
Letterheads, 81,101
Lewis, Dr David, 15
Listening, 71–5,128
Locke, John, 53,55
Logos, 81,101
Lombroso, Cesare, 32,53

Machiavelli, Niccolo, 64
Management, 12,16–20,30,
    62–76,85–90; buy outs,
    67,68
Marco Polo, 98–9
Market Research Society,
    133

Marketing, 66–7,81,108
Marplan, 131
Master/servant role, 44
Maturity, 29,48
Mayo, Prof Elton, 30
Measurement, 87–91
Minorities, 31–2,48–51
Moore, G. E., 65
Morale, 67,69,84
Morality, 52–61,65
MORI, 127,131
Motivation, 84–8,102
Multinationals, 53,81–2

Nissan, 86
Nolan, Vincent, 93
Notice-boards, 95

Objectives, company,
  25,27,69, 81,155;
  individual, 12,27

Packaging, product, 5,82,
  109–10,129
Panic, 143–4
Peer group relationship,
  44–5
Phillips, Gerald M., 75
Philosophy, 52–6,159
Point of sale material, 115
Positioning, in-store, 109–10
Positioning statements,
  81–4, 101,110
Politics, company, 27,64,
  67–9,81
Posture, 36,37
Pragmatism, 15,54
Praise, 69–71
Prejudices, 49–51
Press, 111,115–16,135,
  146–8; trade, 81,
  112–16,119
Press Association, 148,149
Productivity, 29,59–60,69,85
Profits, 127

Promotions, 108,110,
  115–16,119
Psychoanalysis, 14–15
Psychographics, 132–3
Public relations, 8,9,62,
  78–83, 111–12,115,
  118–21,129,130, 155
Purchasing behaviour, 82

Quality circles, 84,94
Quality control, 5,85

Racism, 50
'Rap sessions', 73
Recognition, 69–71
Redundancy, 97,144
Regression, 74
Research, 8,83,127–40;
  market, 108–10,112,131;
  on people, 44–5
Research and development,
  110
Resignation, 73
Retailing,
  100,110,112,115,148
Retzius, Anders, 32
Reward, 140
Robens, Lord, 13

Sales conferences, 120–1
Scottish Business Insider, 62
Sears, R. R., 75
Secretaries/PAs, 46–7
Self-awareness, 5,9–12,
  14–24, 75–6,93;
  organisation, 62–76
Sexuality, 141
Shareholders,
  9,27,78,80,127,129,135
Small talk, 41,45–6
Snobbery, 47; inverted,
  43,47–8
Socrates, 9
Speechwriting/making,
  124–6

Sperry, Roger W., 41
Sponsorship, 112
Spouses, 42,43
Stereotyping, national,
  49–51
Strikes, 59,144
Sublimation, character,
  9–10,13, 156
Submissiveness, 9–10,
  39–40,44,156
Supervisors, 73,86
Suppliers, 9,79,81,100
SWOT analysis, 114–15
Synectics, 118

Takeovers, 67
Targets, 69,81,86,87,140
Teamwork analysis, 21–3,30
Team Briefings, 85–6,88
Time management, 93–4
Trade unions, 58–60,86,138
Training, 5,8,86,102,139

USA, 10–11,15,30,31,35,
  43–4, 155,157
Utilitarianism, 53

VALS, 132
Videos, 31,96–7
Voltaire, 53

Wasey-Campbell-Ewald, 51
Whyte, William H., Jnr, 30
Winch, Dr Robert, 44
Women, 36,42,48,65
Working mothers, 48,65
World War, First, 63;
  Second, 58–60;
Writing, creative, 121–6

Youth culture, 10–11

Zeisel, Hans, 30
Zunin, Leonard and Natalie,
  31